INTERCONNECTED SYSTEMS

EMMANUEL ADEWUSI

INTERCONNECTED SYSTEMS

A WISDOM MANUAL

CCCG Publishing House

CONTENTS

Dedication
ix
Preface
xi
Introduction
xiii

1 — The Need for Systems
1

2 — System Components: People
11

3 — System Components: Process
19

4 — System Component: Technology
27

5 — System Components: Governance
33

6 — Characteristics of a Healthy System
44

7 — Firewalling the System
54

CONTENTS

8 — How to Thrive in a System
64

9 — Demonic Systems
73

10 — Success Systems
79

Epilogue
93
Contact the Author
95
A Sinner's Prayer
97
About the Author
99

Copyright © 2022 Emmanuel Adewusi

All rights reserved. No part of this book may be used or reproduced by any means, graphics, electronic, or mechanical, including photocopying, recording, taping, or by any information storage retrieval system without the author's written permission except in cases of brief quotations embodied in critical articles and reviews.

Scriptures are taken from New King James Version. Copyright 1979, 1980, 1982 by Thomas Nelson, Inc. Used by permission. All right reserved.

Author: Emmanuel Adewusi

ISBN: 978-1-989099-07-0 (hardcover)
ISBN: 978-1-989099-08-7 (ebook)

First Printing, 2022

DEDICATION

I am grateful to my Heavenly Father, Jesus Christ, and the person of the Holy Spirit for the ability to receive and complete this very important assignment. Making a contribution such as this to mankind is not something I take for granted.

I also owe gratitude to my book writing team for their time and effort in meticulously editing this work. May God bless you all.

To my lovely wife, Ibukun Adewusi, thank you for always being dependable, reliable, and selfless in ensuring that kingdom work is done with excellence.

To everyone looking to make the world a better place by building the right systems, I applaud your efforts.

PREFACE

In His infinite wisdom, God created Apostles, Prophets, Pastors, Evangelists, and Teachers, with the sole purpose that each office would add unique value to the body of Christ. Each office plays a vital role in the perfection of the saints for ministry work (Ephesians 4:11-16).

Value can only be added to a person, place, or thing (system) when it comes from a place of strength. This book takes an apostolic perspective to explore the core strength of the apostolic office and gifting, which is the ability to build systems sustainably. When we speak of apostles, the first thought that typically comes to mind is that "they are natural leaders," but have you ever stopped to think why that is? I have realized it is because deeply seated in their leadership ability is the capacity to implement structure and maintain sustainability. Why else would anyone follow a person who seems to lack structure and sustainability in conducting and managing themselves? It is within the nature of an apostle to reason like a computer. They are systematic thinkers. Systems add colour to the world of an apostle. In an environment where systems are non-existent or undermined, an apostle is like a fish out of water. The world is balanced when effective systems are adopted. Resources last, energy is preserved, and value is added continually. Anything that holds value at its core cannot be without a system if it intends to last for an extended period. Take, for example, your life and health. Even though the Bible says you will be blessed with long life, for this to manifest, you must consistently eat right, exercise, and generally

PREFACE

implement the right self-care routines. Determining to eat right is not enough until you put systems in place that will make sure you eat right most, if not all the time.

For everyone who has identified as an apostle or has yet to discover their God-ordained place in the kingdom, I pray this book inspires you! This book will also add value to pastors, teachers, evangelists, and prophets. Through the help of the Holy Spirit, the wisdom from this book will empower you to take charge within the body of Christ and in the secular world. Friend, if you have been charged with an assignment apostolic in nature, this book is for you! If you are serving in a ministry or working within an organization that may be causing you frustration and you feel too handicapped to bring about change, read this book before you jump ship. You will NO MORE struggle to develop and manage systems in the name of Jesus! You will begin to thrive within your workplace, government, ministry, and financial systems!

INTRODUCTION

Six questions are crucial to unlocking dominion in your area of calling. The questions are how, when, what, where, who and why. This book attempts to answer the question of "how?". This question implies the need for clarity and, more specifically, direction regarding how to achieve a goal. The question of "how?" is the first pivotal step to breaking into dominion. Those within the apostolic office are naturally gifted in answering this question. Through the visionary lens of an apostle, we see the strategic placement of people, processes, technology, and governance to achieve a vision.

The day I was enlightened to this reality, it was as if lightning struck twice in the same place. As one in the office of an apostle, my life has never been the same since receiving this revelation. I remember conversing with my Spiritual father in his office in the U.S. in 2018. During that conversation with him, he casually made mention of the word "systems." I tell you, in all truth, it was like my mind exploded, and a sudden rush of revelation flooded into my spirit. The Holy Spirit began to download the concept of "systems" to me. It brought me into a completely different realm.

He continued to break down this new idea to me. After this experience, I realized that everything could be broken down into a system for easy understanding and efficient replication. The presence of a system is evidence of wisdom at work. Can you imagine the frustration of going to Heathrow airport in the United Kingdom to catch a flight, arriving at the airport only to realize that the airport has removed all directional signs and designated

INTRODUCTION

gates for arrival and departure? This will most likely cause confusion as you attempt to navigate through the airport. Friend, you can be sure you would either miss your flight or end up in South America while desiring to land in North America. Many peoples' lives are like this example. When there is no system in place, value cannot be consistently generated.

Systems help to keep the world around us from becoming one giant catastrophe. I once came across a video clip that caught my attention. This clip was of a Pastor who made an altar call to minister to people who needed prayer for healing. In response to the altar call, people flooded toward the altar to be prayed for, in no particular order. As he laid hands on them, many fell under the anointing, and manifestations occurred. Suddenly, he could no longer easily get around from person to person because of the many slain in the spirit on the ground. Watching this video, I could see this was an obvious challenge. To pray for more people, the man of God began stepping over people and mistakenly stepped on someone. Although I would have handled this differently, with the help of the Holy Spirit, I realized it was a teaching moment for me.

The Holy Spirit then leaned in to ask me a question. He spoke, saying, "how many people do you think he would have been able to minister to if he had coordinated the altar call in a more organized manner?". I perceived this was a rhetorical question designed to capture my attention and help me learn. I responded with "I don't know" and remained quiet, waiting for him to shed light on the answer. This incident was another moment of epiphany that exposed me to the idea that a lot more can be accomplished when there is order because the right system has been instituted.

When Jesus wanted to feed the multitude that numbered about five thousand men, not including women and children, He told them to sit on the grass in groups.

INTRODUCTION

> *Then He commanded them to make them all sit down in groups on the green grass. So they sat down in ranks, in hundreds and in the fifties. And when He had taken the five loaves and the two fish, He looked up to heaven, blessed and broke the loaves, and gave them to His disciples to set before them; and the two fish He divided among them all. So they all ate and were filled.* (Mark 6:39-42)

Jesus understood that the five loaves and two fish would only be enough if the people were organized. Jesus would not have fed the people if they were a rowdy bunch. It was not just the anointing Jesus carried or the prayer He prayed that caused the bread and fish to multiply. It was also the organization that was put in place that ensured that Jesus' prayer was answered. When you implement a system in preparation for blessing, you are demonstrating to God that you believe He will show up accordingly.

I pray that God fills your heart and mind with wisdom for identifying and applying systems as you read this book in Jesus' name.

THE NEED FOR SYSTEMS

What is a System?

A system can be described in several ways. The Merriam-Webster dictionary defines it as an organized set of doctrines, ideas, or principles intended to explain the arrangement or workings of an established procedure. From personal exploration and discovery, I define a system as the strategic arrangement of people, processes, technology, and governance to achieve a central purpose. For a system to be effective on all fronts, the right people must be strategically chosen and placed, the process clearly outlined, technology must be efficient, and governance must be sound. When all these moving parts are correctly aligned, you will have for yourself a well-oiled machine.

I guarantee that whenever you see an organization thriving or a person that has achieved consistent success in life, it is because they have intentionally implemented a success system. An adequate system is laced with wisdom. Show me a well-thought-out system, and I'll point out the spirit of wisdom behind it.

The world we live in is established on systems. For example, the American military can only be as powerful and thriving as it is because of effective systems put in place for strategic battle tactics. America is known as a military superpower today primarily because of the systems in place to ensure its armed forces achieve the sole purpose of defending the nation's territorial integrity and interests against adversaries. It is incredible to think that the safety and security of an entire country are practically dependent on implementing an effective defence system. That is billions of lives at stake!

A few years ago, the Holy Spirit told me that a genuine trailblazer allows God to show them a pattern that is then birthed here on earth. True originality can only come from God. Let me also mention that knowing what to do is not the same as knowing when to do it. Wisdom is multifaceted and should be employed tactfully to yield the right results. According to Ecclesiastes 10:15, "The labour of fools wearies them, for they do not even know how to go to the city!" You will no longer be seen as a fool in Jesus' name because the wisdom of God will show you how to get to your destination.

Another way to understand the principle of a system is to think of a motor vehicle. Many parts factor into a safe, effective, and sustainable vehicle. These parts are members brought together to establish a system that allows the car to run smoothly and accomplish its purpose of transporting individuals from one location to another. However, when broken down into its parts, one can see the wisdom in each component coming together to form a functioning system. The reverse definition of a system can be taken from this example, in the sense that any object or process that can be broken down into distinct parts is systematic. When pieced together, it can carry out a purposeful function.

In the Beginning

If we are to grasp the genius in the concept of systems, we must first understand the genius of creation and its beginning. The Alpha and Omega of creation tells us a story in Genesis 1:1-5 of the earth in a void, formless and deeply dark state. At a moment's notice, God spoke life into the void and a system for life was created. What you and I call earth today is made up of separate parts that create a habitation for human, animal, and plant life when put together. All of which are interconnected and dependent on each other to thrive.

Genesis chapter one has become a scripture I refer to when faced with a seemingly challenging situation. I have discovered much wisdom in the breakdown of the story of creation, or rather, the story of interconnected systems. With Genesis chapter one stored in my spirit, I can confidently say that EVERY SINGLE PROBLEM HAS A SOLUTION. Before creating the earth, God was faced with three challenges, the challenge of formlessness, emptiness, and darkness. In Genesis 1:2, we see that the earth was without form and void and everywhere was covered in darkness.

Formless and empty is usually how a structure looks before a system is established. I'm sure God looked and said, "Hmm, a few things are missing here," and immediately saw the possibility of the earth taking shape. God saw what it could be before he began the process of restructuring. He first started by separating the waters and creating the atmosphere. The bible calls this atmosphere Heaven, and everything under the atmosphere He called the earth.

He then separated the body of water from the dry land. After he did all this, God began to fill the earth, starting with plant life and continuing onto animal life. Humans were next in God's creation plan, and He designed them to be the spitting image of Himself. Finally, at the latter end of this chapter, we see God's attention shift from creating to maintaining what He had created.

From this entire chapter, we can see the entirety of what a system is all about.

From what we saw God do initially, it is evident that you need a vision of the end from the beginning. You need to identify the connections between each element in the system, and you also need to factor in the system's sustainability. In essence, God is the originator of systems. The Bible is filled with many examples and stories of God Himself and great men and women He raised to operate in divine wisdom to establish systems. To a large extent, the governing system of the world today is grounded on systems long established in the Bible.

King Solomon's System

Another glaring system in the Bible was built by Solomon when he erected the temple of God and the king's palace. When we observe the early stages of Solomon's life, we see a man that demonstrated wisdom in a unique and sophisticated way. In 1 Kings 10:1-9, we see how Solomon uniquely displayed wisdom.

> *Now when the queen of Sheba heard of the fame of Solomon concerning the name of the Lord, she came to test him with hard questions. She came to Jerusalem with a very great retinue, with camels that bore spices, very much gold, and precious stones; and when she came to Solomon, she spoke with him about all that was in her heart. So Solomon answered all her questions; there was nothing so difficult for the king that he could not explain it to her. And when the queen of Sheba had seen all the wisdom of Solomon, the house that he had built, the food on his table, the seating of his servants, the service of his waiters and their apparel, his cupbearers, and his entryway by which he went up to the house of the Lord, there was no more spirit in her. Then she said to the king: "It was a true report which I heard in my own*

> *land about your words and your wisdom. However, I did not believe the words until I came and saw with my own eyes; and indeed the half was not told me. Your wisdom and prosperity exceed the fame of which I heard. Happy are your men and happy are these your servants, who stand continually before you and hear your wisdom! Blessed be the Lord your God, who delighted in you, setting you on the throne of Israel! Because the Lord has loved Israel forever, therefore He made you king, to do justice and righteousness."*

We know that it was in his words and how he creatively organized things in his palace. The queen of Sheba was so amazed that the Bible even says that "there was no more spirit in her." (1 Kings 10:5) I can imagine how many jaw-dropping oo's and ahh's she must have uttered in admiration of such wisdom.

What exactly did Queen Sheba see? The Bible tells us that she saw the wisdom of Solomon. (1 Kings 10:6-8) This wisdom manifested in the way Solomon built the palace that he occupied. The food arrangement on his table, the way he sat, and his servants' clothing were all centered around the theme of beauty. Thus, bringing our attention to the idea that every system has a theme.

I can imagine that when the architect came to show him the blueprint for the palace, Solomon emphasized the need for a "wow" factor! Demanding that it be as grand as possible, with the best of the best! I can imagine the sculptor bringing a silver sculpture of a lion and Solomon's response being, "why is this not in gold like I asked!" According to 1 Kings 3, Solomon's ability to establish an enduring system for his kingdom was rooted in the wisdom he received from God. A system answers how a thing should be done, hence why you can never have an enduring system without wisdom.

The way he arranged his administration ensured that he did not suffer any loss, and his resources continued to multiply. He assured that his administration properly accounted for spiritual matters, defence, the economy, and other vital aspects of his kingly duties; of note is the account in 1 Kings 4:7. Solomon had twelve governors over the nation who provided food for the king and his household for one month each year. Another interesting thing is that in 1 Kings 4:28, Solomon ensured that the governors that made provisions each month brought the barley and straw to a predetermined place for his horses and steeds.

It was not enough for them to provide for the king's needs each month. The system also dictated where they brought the provision, how much they got and who looked after it. May God endow you with wisdom to build suitable systems in Jesus' name.

Joseph's System

Joseph was another man in scripture who displayed wisdom in setting up his system. When Joseph appeared before Pharaoh and interpreted his dream, what caught Pharoah's attention was the system Joseph proposed for solving the impending famine. Joseph told Pharaoh to find the right person, implement the proper process, build the right technology to house the excess grain, and apply the appropriate governance techniques to secure Egypt's future for the years to come.

In Genesis 41: 33-36 (emphasis added), we see the breakdown of this proposed system.

> *Now, therefore, let Pharaoh select a discerning and wise man and set him over the land of Egypt (people and governance). Let Pharaoh do this, and let him appoint officers over the land, to collect one-fifth of the produce of the land of Egypt in the seven great years (People and process). And let them gather all the food of those good years that are coming, and store up grain under the authority of Pharaoh, and let them keep food in the cities (People, process, technology, and governance). Then that food shall be as a reserve for the land*

for the seven years of famine which shall be in the land of Egypt that the land may not perish during the famine.

No wonder the Bible said that Pharaoh was very impressed with the recommendation Joseph gave because there is no sense in having a process without the right person to manage it, nor is there any value in having any other system component without the others. This validates the idea that a system cannot function maximally without all the components in place. In essence, it must be all or nothing. What God showed Pharaoh revealed that there would be a time of plenty and a time of lack. Our Heavenly Father is a God of times and seasons. If you allow God to give you hints of what is coming, you'll always be prepared and understand the ways and movements of God.

God covered every aspect in this instance with Joseph and Pharaoh. Joseph was walking in prudence because God gave him the ability to see ahead. As a result, the advice Joseph gave was good in Pharaoh's eyes. Everything we have right now is enough to take care of all we need, but we must always have a system in place to help maximize our resources to achieve our goals. When you don't put a system in place, you are left with the option of making emotionally driven decisions.

You are left to operate by chance. There is no way to continually succeed when operating by chance. Wisdom is beautiful, and there is a lot to be admired when wisdom is at work.

The State of Israel

Another system of note that could arguably be one of the most significant other than creation is the establishment of the state of Israel. After God delivered the children of Israel from the bondage of Egypt, He immediately presented a system by which they would be governed. God knew that delivering the Israelites from Pharaoh was not enough and that they needed a system if they were going to survive as a nation and remain free. After rescuing them from over 400 years of slavery, God began by appointing people to fulfil specific roles in the newly formed nation. For example, the priesthood was established, leadership roles in families were ratified, etc.

God then began to show them how to run their society. For example, He taught them about justice, marriage, worship, work, etc. God also taught them about technology, which included acceptable materials for creating different things. For example, materials for building the temple, anointing oil, and many others. Finally, God established a governing system that tied all three components together.

This system had God at the very top as the King of Israel. God pays extreme attention to systems, as the Bible says, "If the foundation is destroyed, what can the righteous do?" (Psalms 11:3). My translation of Psalms 11:3 is, "if the system is faulty, what can the righteous do." At the root of perpetual bondage is a rigged system. Hence why God was frequently displeased with the children of Israel and how they lived their lives.

One of the ways that God shows His love for His children is by giving them insight into systems they can put in place for continued success. Psalm 103:7 tells us that God exposed Moses to His ways, which is why he was not only able to lead the children of Israel out of Egypt, but he also played a significant role in showing them what they can do to maintain their freedom. It does not matter if you like the State of Israel or not. There is no denying that they are a force to be reckoned with worldwide. Even though sworn enemies surround them, Israel remains a tiny nation in size but practically indestructible. This systematic approach is not limited to God's kingdom, and even the devil utilizes a systems approach.

Demonic Systems

Jesus gave us insight into how the devil operates his kingdom in Matthew 12:22-30.

> Then one was brought to Him who was demon-possessed, blind and mute; and He healed him so that the blind and mute man both spoke and saw. And all the multitudes were amazed and said, "Could this be the Son of David?" Now when the Pharisees heard it, they said, "This fellow does not cast out demons except by Beelzebub, the ruler of the demons." But Jesus knew their thoughts and said to them: "Every kingdom divided against itself is brought to desolation, and every city or house divided against itself will not stand. If Satan casts out Satan, he is divided against himself. How then will his kingdom stand? And if I cast out demons by Beelzebub, by whom do your sons cast them out? Therefore, they shall be your judges. But if I cast out demons by the Spirit of God, surely the kingdom of God has come upon you. Or how can one enter a strong man's house and plunder his goods, unless he first binds the strong man? And then he will plunder his house. He who is not with Me is against Me, and he who does not gather with Me scatters abroad.

Since that kingdom is still operational today, we can assume that it has an established system keeping it afloat. In verse 26, Jesus confirmed that the devil has a kingdom. In verse 24, the Pharisees referred to Beelzebub as a ruler or demon, like a chief of staff. Even though all satan's minions are classified as demons, they technically either function as foot soldiers, principalities, powers, rulers of darkness, or spiritual hosts of wickedness in heavenly places. In Ephesians 6:12, the Bible gives us a snapshot of the governance structure of the kingdom of darkness.

In the demonic system, the demons and their captives form the people aspect of the system. The process aspect of the demonic system shows how the devil captures people and keeps them in captivity using temptation and other means from generation to generation. According to the scriptures, the devil employs wiles or tricks. Deception is an example of one of the technologies that the enemy uses to perpetuate theft, murder, and destruction.

Another example of technology the enemy employs in gathering and housing his captives includes homes and religious centers fed with lies to keep them bound. Finally, the governance aspect of the demonic system involves the devil at the top and then spiritual hosts of wickedness, rulers of the darkness of this age, powers, and principalities. Note that all these demonic influences can only operate on earth through people. According to the way God established the earth, no one can exist on the earth without a body to operate through. An understanding of this principle is the root of lasting deliverance.

In each of these examples we have discussed, you will notice that every viable, sustainable system has four things in common. They have people, processes, governance, and technology. From our example, at the beginning, where God created the heavens and the earth, you will see that people were involved. Man oversaw governance, and the technology for creation was the word and the Spirit of God. We will be exploring these in detail in the following chapters.

The wisdom that comes from God speaks for itself, and wherever you identify wisdom, rest assured that it is anchored in a deliberate system. In the same way, the evidence of wisdom can be seen in all shapes and styles, and a lack of it can also easily be pointed out. For instance, you can observe an individual from their dressing and immediately know if they are walking in wisdom. I have seen youth in the cool of winter waiting by transit stations wearing shorts and a t-shirt. I could tell that wisdom was a scarce virtue in their life at that time.

I have concluded that wisdom and a structured system are essential to one's ability to thrive in every area of life.

SYSTEM COMPONENTS: PEOPLE

Guiding Principles

Every system component has guiding principles by which they must operate. The people component of a system has four guiding principles.

Principle 1: Everyone is unique
Principle 2: Everyone has a place
Principle 3: Everyone must have a voice
Principle 4: Everyone has a skill

Wisdom can be displayed in the arrangement of people. Ephesians 4:7-11 depicts how we can demonstrate wisdom in the body of Christ through the arrangement of people. Concerning the church, God set a system for administering dominion through the five-fold offices. Each child of God either falls in the office of a pastor, teacher, apostle, evangelist, or prophet. For the body of Christ to function at its best, each child in the kingdom must take their rightful place. An apostle would stand firm in the grace for leadership, and a prophet would communicate the will of God at every point in time. An evangelist would market the kingdom's message, a pastor would shepherd their sheep, and a teacher would accurately communicate and defend the word of God.

The Apostle governs; the prophet guides; the evangelist gathers; the pastor guards, while the teacher grounds. The Apostle leads; the prophet speaks; the teacher equips; the evangelist proclaims, and the pastor cares. The Apostle is the visionary strategist; the prophet the spiritual advisor; the teacher is the logical thinker; the evangelist is the persuasive communicator, while the pastor is the human resource specialist. The Apostle has farsight; the prophet has foresight; the evangelist has hindsight; the teacher has insight, and the pastor has oversight. The Apostle provides the mission; the prophet receives the vision; the evangelist spreads the passion; the pastor displays compassion, and the teacher details the commission. Finally, the Apostle is the brain; the prophet operates the five senses; the evangelist provides the muscles; the pastor is the skeletal system, and the teacher is the immune system.

When you see a company like Amazon thriving, one reason is that they have a better system than their competitors. Many other companies sell things online, but none have a system as effective as Amazon's. A system will show if wisdom is at work in a place or not and what kind of wisdom is at work there.

It is high time that the body of Christ appreciates wisdom. Wherever the wisdom of God is, there is glory. Likewise, wherever shame resides, wisdom is lacking. However, it does not mean that God is not there, but rather that someone did not pay attention to the wisdom that creates increase. A system is the only sustainable way to be faithful in whatever you're given, and it shows how an assignment can be done with excellence.

The only way Joseph was able to excel was because of the system he put in place. Anything of value that is not in an intentional system will be lost. Without wisdom, a system cannot be created and sustained. The number of chapters devoted to documenting the deliverance of the children of Israel from Egypt pales in comparison to the books and chapters in the Bible detailing how the nascent nation of Israel should be governed. These systems were needed for Israel to be a mighty nation.

Without wisdom and systems, the children of Israel would not have been able to sustain the deliverance God gave them in their new nation. When you hear about God's principles and commands, understand that he speaks with systems in mind. A system operates the way a habit works, and once put in place, it functions until tampered with.

Right People

Solomon was king, and all these were his officials (1 Kings 4:1-2); my question to you is, who are your officials or associates? Have you selected them, or have they picked you? The Bible then begins to list them. We see that the wisest man of that time even had advisors; who are the ones advising you? Many people are speaking around you, but who are you intentionally listening to?

In 1 Kings chapter 4, we see wisdom demonstrated in the way people were strategically positioned to take care of various responsibilities. When effective systems are at work, life's administrative tasks can be taken care of without thinking about them; all you must do is think of creative things.

When you look at the different systems in the body, you see a combination of other things functioning together to achieve a goal, which is to keep the entire body alive and functioning. So, wherever you have wisdom, you have a system. And the better the wisdom, the better the system. Now let's discuss the people component of every system.

People are critical for the day-to-day operations of a system. The actual harvest comes when the right people function in the right places. Genesis 2:4-6 emphasizes the need for people.

> *This is the history of the heavens and the earth when they were created, on the day that the Lord God made the earth and the heavens, before any plant of the field was in the earth and before any herb of the field had grown. For the Lord God had not caused it to rain on the earth, and there was no man to till the ground, but a mist went up from the earth and watered the whole face of the ground.*

We see that God could not bring an increase without the right people to manage it. Hence, God only released mist to water the plants before man was created. In Genesis 2:7, God caused rain to fall after He created man and placed him in the garden to do the work he was assigned to do. The book of revelation chapter five also gives us insight into God's thought process when he was seeking who was worthy to open the scroll.

The correct positions and assignments must be given to the right people. The Bible records a council meeting in heaven where God asked who could open this scroll, and we know that Jesus answered that call. Hence, God has always searched for the right people for every kingdom-related assignment. God also seeks intercessors who can stand in the gap to ensure that people are not destroyed.

> *So I sought for a man among them who would make a wall, and stand in the gap before Me on behalf of the land, that I should not destroy it; but I found no one.* (Ezekiel 22:30)

In the case of King Saul, God replaced him because he was no longer in alignment with God's plan and went to seek out David, a humble, good-looking shepherd after His own heart. He sought Paul even though Paul's mission was previously to attack the church.

Right Place

It is critical to note here that a healthy system must have a human resource department that has systems in place for soliciting, triaging, and disseminating feedback received from the people within the system. The former are reasons why every organization has a human resource department. And as you can expect, their job is to hire the right people, retain them, and ensure that each person's voice is heard.

There is value in accurately identifying people and assigning them to specific responsibilities. People can be identified based on their personality, character, and who or what influences them. Their personality is who God made them be; character is who they have become, while who or what influences them will determine who they will eventually evolve to be. You must learn to discern people based on what is in their hearts and what is in their hands. What is in their heart represents their idea of who they are, while what is in their hands reflects who they have already become. What is in the heart is futuristic in nature but what is in their hands is current. Most people have an inaccurate understanding of who they are. They either over or underestimate themselves.

It is a mistake to staff people based on who they want to be alone. To avoid disappointment, only put people in positions after what they have in their hearts has manifested as reality in their hands.

Right Personality

Let's start with how to identify the right personality for a task. I know what you might be thinking, but there should never be the right personality. The truth, however, is that there is an ideal personality for every task. There are many tools available that can be used to do this. One tool commonly used to assess personality types is the 5-factor model. This tool has five categories explaining human personality aspects: openness, extraversion, conscientiousness, neuroticism, and agreeableness.

Another widely used tool for identifying people's personalities is the four-temperament model. The temperaments in the four temperament models are: Sanguine, Choleric, Melancholy, Phlegmatic. Alternatively, you can use the colours as made famous in the Colorful Personalities book by George Boelcke as a basis for identifying each person's unique personality. The different personality types in Colorful Personalities are blue, orange, green, and gold.

The colourful personalities book popularized the concept of personality types through colours. The blue personality type thrives in relationships and builds strong connections with people. They have a strong ability to make everyone around them feel special and accepted.

The green personality type will naturally take the lead in any project type environment, and they have an insatiable appetite for knowledge and personal growth. Their world is made up of facts and opinions. The orange personality type will brighten up your day with their buoyant attitude and optimistic perspective on life. They are the "life of the party" but can often be the last to arrive. The gold personality type is strongly motivated by their sense of duty and responsibility. They usually go above and beyond in helping and supporting others.

Personalities come in all shapes and sizes. Understanding the unique traits each person carries will help you identify their strengths and give them responsibilities and positions within their capacity for your peace of mind. Ephesians 4:7-11 emphasizes the importance of utilizing and placing people within their natural areas of gifting.

Rightly Yoked

I have found that many people have a narrow understanding of the instruction not to be unequally yoked (2 Corinthians 6:14). The mistake they make is that they often limit it to romantic relationships, which is very incorrect! This instruction extends to the idea that for your success to happen, the system that the other party is under must match with your system. Think of the process you go through when donating blood to someone.

For your body to accept another person's blood, you need to have compatible blood. Likewise, while every human being can potentially be good, not every potentially good human being is compatible with your system. Hence, putting people in the right place within your system is essential.

How do we choose the right people?

Choosing the right people comes down to three things: Experience, Expectation and Evolution. Think of these guiding principles as qualities an employer would list in a job description for new hires. In determining the right people, you would want to start by asking a few questions that will help validate the potential prospects. "Do the potential prospects for this assignment have previous experience in this area?", "Do the potential prospects have valuable background knowledge in what I am aiming to achieve?", "Do the potential prospect's experience and performance exemplify the level of excellence I am currently looking for?". These guiding questions will help set the tone of your search.

Some organizations can measure and validate expectations by getting their staff to sign agreements. To measure expectations, begin to zoom in on those that have agreed to walk with you (Amos 3:3), and have bought into your vision. These individuals are the ones with whom you must share the same expectation when it comes to standards, core values, quality, and character.

Evolution looks at an individual's ability to be taught, transform, and get better over time. It examines a person's response to change while adapting and learning in changing environments.

When we look at a mighty man like Moses, we see that God could teach him and expose him to miracles and wonders that had never been done before. Why? Simply because Moses was a man with a teachable spirit. Change was a process he readily stepped into. Moses was able to evolve into what God needed him to be. As God led and instructed, he moved.

SYSTEM COMPONENTS: PROCESS

Guiding Principles

The process component of a system has four guiding principles.

Principle 1: Every task must have a procedure
Principle 2: Every procedure must be documented
Principle 3: Every procedure must be efficiently completed by a qualified person
Principle 4: Every procedure can be improved

You can never achieve anything lasting by leaving things to chance. In establishing a sustainable system, one must intentionally set and strategically place things. Only then will the system function and thrive on its own. A clearly defined process secures a system, and wisdom is at the foundation of such a system. A process answers the questions, "what do we do and how do we do it?

The administration of King Solomon is one to be admired! It was unparalleled in strategy. The first key to note from 1 Kings 4:1-28 is that in all of Solomon's abundance, he took steps to ensure he assigned officials to assist him in managing his administration. The burden of management was shared across his officials. Solomon exuded stress-free excellence. He placed people in the correct positions to get the work done. There is no stress when wisdom is at work. The more straightforward the process, the easier it will be to execute. Focus on what you want to achieve, not the tools used. In this section, however, we will examine the need for utilizing the right processes.

In 1 Kings 5:12-38, Solomon raised a labour force to work in the land. He ensured that everything was managed correctly, from building a temple to its successful completion. Under Solomon's rule, people knew what they were responsible for. Though he spent seven years building the temple, the temple was completed with excellence. Processes help to complete a project or assignment in a timely manner. Whenever something is going to take time, a process must be intentionally implemented. Once the right people are in place, the next step is to determine what needs to be done and document it so others can follow along. Gideon told his three hundred soldiers to watch him and do what they saw him do.

> *And he said to them, "Look at me and do likewise; watch, and when I come to the edge of the camp you shall do as I do.* (Judges 7:17)

These men observed Gideon's process for engaging in battle and followed accordingly. Here Gideon showed the three hundred men the process of how to fight and win that battle. A process can be explained as the proper way to do something. In the absence of an approved process, people are left to their own devices, which will end up becoming a mishmash of different things. There are many ways to come up with the proper process. A recommended approach is to brainstorm with a team of qualified individuals rather than one individual. Another method is to review how others in the same situation have approached the same problem to avoid reinventing the wheel.

As you read what God did through Solomon, may He build in you the desire to put proper processes in place to execute your assignment. When Queen Sheba came in to see the arrangement of Solomon's palace, she was in awe (1 Kings 10:4-9). I believe this was when she fell in love with Solomon. When given an assignment, use wisdom to arrange things so that the assignment can be consistently executed with excellence. Continuous excellence is impossible in an environment where the process is unclear. This is what wisdom can do.

When thinking about the ideal process and how it should be laid out, remember that each process has a theme it represents. The theme of a process is determined by the goal a process must achieve. The theme behind Solomon's system was excellence and beauty. Some processes must be made with functionality in mind. A waste management system perhaps should be implemented with functionality rather than beauty as the theme. Determine what theme is ideal for your process.

Excellence vs Perfection

A process is developed by thinking about the big picture and breaking it into manageable chunks. Imagine you were asked to eat an elephant (don't try this at home); how would you go about it? I assume you would start from a logical place, possibly the mid stomach area, until all that remains are bones.

One of the major hindrances to developing a process is the mindset of perfection. It would be challenging, if not impossible, to create a process with perfection in mind, mainly because perfection is a myth. Whatever would have been the best would have previously been better; what would be better would have been good. What is good might have once been bad.

Systems thinking must be approached from a logical, progressive mindset. To continuously make progress, do your best to start with what you have as quickly as possible. While implementing your process, make it a point to document all the problem spots, inconsistencies, pain points, and natural preferences. This is the principle behind software development approaches. If software developers wait until there are no bugs in their software to release them, we might not have any software systems in use today. Do your due diligence to determine what is absolutely necessary and improve from there onwards.

Sequencing

When counting from 1-10, it is not enough to know that three or perhaps 6 are numbers within this range. Counting from 1-10 is only accurate when the count follows the proper sequence. A process is more effective and efficient when the correct sequence is followed. Here are some things to think about while working on the sequencing of your operations. What arrangement avoids the waste of time? What sequence avoids the waste of materials? What sequence avoids waste of money? What sequence produces an output for the following process?

Follow me to Genesis chapter 1, as we see how the master apostle, our Heavenly Father, sequenced His problem-solving approach. God faced three problems: darkness, emptiness, and lack of structure. The principles for sequencing mentioned earlier can be found in this chapter. It made sense for God to see what he was doing first, so He said, "let there be light." Where there is no light, there would most likely be waste and destruction.

In essence, God intended to fill the earth, but light and structure were necessary prerequisites. The next thing God did was establish structure before filling the earth with valuables. Again, without structure, waste is inevitable. Often people are in haste to fill a void without seeing the need for the unnecessary (mundane) necessities, like light and structure. Without proper sequencing, vain repetition will be the norm. Are you finding it hard to retain blessings? Perhaps, you need to first seek the light (understanding) and put structure in place to retain the blessings.

Ecclesiastes chapter three makes the essence of the time factor known to us. Every good and beautiful work under heaven has a time to manifest its exact value and purpose. When we align the systems we put in place with God's timing, it positions it for greater heights and success. The sons of Issachar were aligned with God's timing for when their understanding of times and seasons was to manifest.

The devil is not to jealously establish a manipulated version of every good and perfect thing that God does. The devil prides himself in the ability to pre-maturely offer someone a "good thing" but in a non-sequential manner. He does this to take them out of God's perfect timing (Proverbs 14:12). There are ways to avoid falling into this trap, and a wise person would know when to take specific steps. This is where one should ask God, what should I do first? When should I do this or that?

Make it Plain

After your process has been thoughtfully laid out from start to finish, you must now document it. It is essential to document the process you have decided on, even though it should undergo regular changes. It is vital to take note of the process you have decided on, even though this process should still undergo frequent changes. In Habakkuk 2:4, we are told to write the vision and make it plain. Do you realize that loaded in every vision is a series of steps leading to the desired destination? You can decide the way to capture this process. Some processes are better captured in video format, while others are best captured in written form. Some processes are better captured in detail, while others are better captured as step-by-step checklists. A hybrid approach consisting of video, written, detailed or concise steps is ideal in some environments.

We establish processes in preparation for new opportunities. Premeditated processes have the potential to yield excellent results. A deliberate process has all the steps to achieve a goal mapped out before anything officially starts. Many people run away from developing a process because the effort requires brainpower to formulate. This kind of response is the quickest way to a failed effort; it is like investing time and effort into something just for it to fail because you neglected to put a system in place.

Have you ever gone to multiple locations of the same restaurant and received the same service and food quality? If yes, you should know that quality customer and food service was replicated because of their well-thought process. The steps outlined in a process establish order, leading to an increase.

Proverbs 6:6 urges us to study the ants and observe their natural process for ensuring consistent productivity. When we study the ant, we learn the significance of having a process outlining the steps needed to accomplish a task or goal consistently. If your vision is to start a business, start by asking yourself the question, "what steps do I need to take to start this business." In many cases, you will not have the answer to the question within yourself. In cases where you are unable to personally answer the question of what steps to take, you will have to reach out directly or indirectly to those with the answer. Outline the steps, and there you have it, a process for starting up a business.

You Need the Holy Spirit

Wisdom is just a question or observation away (Proverbs 4:25-26). Wisdom has to do with processes; a significant part of it is rooted in the art of pondering, which can also be understood as brainstorming, meditating, or analyzing. In this scripture, wisdom asks us to consider the direction we want to go and the steps needed to get us there. Ask yourself questions like what steps should I take? I like to ponder the personal experiences of those ahead of me. The wisdom I gain from the many great servants of God I look up to is what I use as a starting point for most of my endeavours. I think from a first-principles perspective in cases where there are no examples to follow. First-principles thinking involves focusing your attention on what matters, that is, the barest minimum steps required to get to where you want to get to.

Oh! How sweet the leading of the Holy Spirit is! The prophet brings us into the secret of what it means to be exposed to the guiding and teaching ministry of the Holy Ghost; this is one of the enjoyable aspects of Him. It is an opportunity to walk hand in hand with the one who has experience in all things. Through this scripture, we see how the farmer follows a step-by-step process.

> *Give ear and hear my voice, listen and hear my speech. Does the plowman keep plowing all day to sow? Does he keep turning his soil and breaking the clods? When he has levelled its surface, does he not sow the black cummin and scatter the cummin, plant the wheat in rows, the barley in the appointed place, and the spelt in its place? For He instructs him in right judgment, his God teaches him. For the black cummin is not threshed with a threshing sled, nor is a cartwheel rolled over the cummin; But the black cummin is beaten out with a stick, and the cummin with a rod. Bread flour must be ground; Therefore he does not thresh it forever, break it with his cartwheel, or crush it with his horsemen. This also comes from*

the Lord of hosts, who is wonderful in counsel and excellent in guidance. (Isaiah 28:23-29)

The advantage we should always be looking for to achieve excellence is not found in common sense steps but rather in the direction of the Holy Spirit. Every child of God has access to this ministry of the Holy Ghost. Many people miss out because of the wrong assumptions they have concerning it. Whatever the reason, it is important to remember that we have the one who has done all things and that there is nothing too difficult for Him to walk you through. The Holy Spirit can give patterns and steps for every area of your life to ensure you are never blindsided.

Isaiah was talking about how the Holy Spirit is wonderful in leading people and his ability to give wise counsel (Isaiah 28:23-29). The giftings and the capabilities we have are essentially useless without the Holy Ghost. The same way a racehorse needs an experienced rider to race well, we need the Holy Spirit to operate at our best capacity. All we simply need to do to experience and enjoy this is to yield to His leading. God does not lead goats; he leads sheep. So, shifting into a yielded mentality is to go from behaving like a goat to following like a sheep.

SYSTEM COMPONENT: TECHNOLOGY

Guiding Principles

Every system component has guiding principles by which they operate. The technology component of a system has four guiding principles.

Principle 1: Everything important should be automated
Principle 2: Everything important should be preserved
Principle 3: Everything important should be multiplied
Principle 4: Everything important should be secured

The purpose of technology is to help with efficiency and effectiveness. From 2 Chronicles 26:1-15, we understand that Uzziah was successful because he sought God, and as a result, God caused him to prosper. In his reign as King, Uzziah built towers and wells. He understood that tools and technology were needed to enhance his kingdom's efficiency. Imagine if he had not built the structures he did, he would not correctly manage the workload he was responsible for. Uzziah was an effective leader because he ran a tight ship and covered his bases. On the military side of things, he had people and implemented a process to govern. On the battlefield, Uzziah had the best weapons. The tools he prepared for war against the enemy were effective because they were designed for combat. Uzziah did not show up to a sword and spear fight with stones but was prepared with the right tools. Skilled men designed these tools, enhancing their ability to war effectively.

Technology helps to simplify a process and enhance human capacity. When a human being connects with technology, he can become an enhanced human. In the kingdom of God, the Holy Spirit is the enhancing factor that man must bind with to become superhuman. As children of God, we have access to the Holy Spirit and his superhuman capability-building strength.

When using technology, you must evaluate if it will make your life easier and assist you in achieving your goals. Think of all the apps on your phone that you use most often. Ask yourself how these things help make your life easier. What is adding value to your life? Are you using these things intentionally? Look at the arrangement of your apps, and ask yourself, are these arranged deliberately? If these things are not appropriately governed, they can set us back. There are different technologies that you can put in place in various aspects of your life. Apps can be used to help you manage your physical health without constantly running to the doctor. Your contacts, reminders and notes app are available tools and can be used to help us achieve our goals. What tools do you use to manage your life? For example, I use an app called notability. I have used this for years now. Its effectiveness has helped me immensely in keeping my notes organized and up to date. It syncs across all my devices. Find time to sit down to identify which tool, apps, technologies you have access to that you can use to manage your life in a way that maximizes your effectiveness in all areas.

Multipliers

One of the roles of technology is to help multiply productivity and impact. Technology, when properly used, is meant to make life easier. Today, technology has advanced so much that practically an app, tool, software, or machine can help get work done. Every field of endeavour now has technology solutions that can either enhance your ability to work faster or improve the quality of work produced. In some cases, you might have to combine multiple software applications to arrive at the perfect solution to get your job done.

When you find yourself engaging in repetitive and mundane tasks, it is time to find a tool to replace your efforts and redeem your time. A few of my favourite apps to use are for managing my calendar, notes, reminders, voice recording and data backup. When choosing apps to enhance my workflow, I typically prefer cloud applications that can be accessed from anywhere instead of applications limited to a computer at a time.

The goal of using technology is so that your workflow is effective and efficient and enables you to get your job done. As you use these tools, ensure that you are not just looking for free apps but rather ones that enhance your work productivity, even if it means you must pay for it.

Automation

Technology can help to save time by capturing information to be replayed multiple times. Technology can help to freeze time through its ability to capture experiences to be viewed in the future. Paper, audio, or video recordings can capture information to help redeem the time. Can you imagine if we did not have the Bible recorded on paper or other formats? Can you imagine how challenging that would have been for Christians to grow closer to Christ? Technology can help enforce or enhance the different system components: people, process, technology, and governance. For example, training can be recorded and made available to future staff members without requiring a team member to keep repeating the same information while training other team members. Technology can augment the capabilities a human being can provide. Technology will ensure the consistency and accuracy of the information passed and communicated within a system. Which of your repeatable processes can be replaced with computer software? Which of your processes can be better handled by software? Which of your processes is riddled with errors, hence should be replaced by computer software?

Data Backup

One of the aspects of technology to pay attention to is your data storage and backup. I have found that people are typically not concerned about data backup until they lose critical information. Choose from the diverse hardware and software options for data backup from what is available based on your cost, access, and security needs. While many cloud-based options like iCloud, google drive, dropbox, etc., are available for frequent and convenient access, I still recommend using portable hard drives as a viable backup. Even though this is now few and far between, there have been times when online options have been inaccessible. Hence, I recommend also having your important information backed up on a hard drive.

Information Security

Classified information should be secured appropriately. When thinking about data security, the trade-off is typically between convenience and security. The more stringent the security is, the less convenient it is to access information, and vice versa. Passwords, fingerprint scanners, and other security tools should be leveraged to protect valuable information. Security is needed because of the confidentiality requirement and the data's integrity and availability requirements. You might think there is no need to secure your information because it is not sensitive, but that is not the right way to view information security. The triads of information security are confidentiality, integrity, and availability.

Confidentiality means that the information is for your eyes only. This security aspect covers sensitive information that you do not want anyone else to see. Tools like passwords help to keep your information from prying eyes. Integrity refers to the accuracy of the information. Some information may not need to be confidential, but it can be damaging if its accuracy is tampered with. Tools like hashing technology and backup help to ensure the integrity of your information. Finally, availability refers to the need for the information to be accessible. Some information may not need to be confidential but must be available 24/7. Cloud technology and backup can help to ensure the availability of your information.

The technology we use can be a blessing when properly used. Take your time to determine your information security needs and secure your information accordingly.

Artificial Intelligence and Robotics

Over the years, I have realized the fast pace at which the world is changing and the growing influence of artificial intelligence. Artificial intelligence is the intelligence built into the software you use. This is where the software can learn how a human being acquires information. Every day artificial intelligence is learning and improving. It learns human habits and adjusts on the fly to copy human behaviour etc. We have reached a point now where artificial intelligence can replace many humans at their job.

A time is coming when many jobs will no longer be in need. Many countries have started experimenting with different alternatives for when human labour is no longer needed—for example, universal wages, where people get paid just for existing. However, God knows the end from the beginning. If you genuinely involve God in the choices you make, He will not set you up. He will surely guide and direct you on a path to ensure that you will always be relevant. As led by the Holy Spirit, you will arrive in a domain that robots can never take over. We have wisdom, and in wisdom, there is knowledge.

SYSTEM COMPONENTS: GOVERNANCE

Guiding Principles

Every system component has guiding principles that they operate by. The governance component of a system has four guiding principles.

Principle 1: Someone must be clearly accountable for every process and technology

Principle 2: Everyone should regularly give account for what they are responsible for

Principle 3: There must be principles, policies, and procedures for utilizing people, processes, and technology.

Principle 4: Everyone must be supervised by someone

When you study the sequence of how God began creation, you will see that certain fundamental aspects needed to be in place before God gave the increase. Many have not begun to experience the rain or harvest God has in store for them because they have no structure in place to manage it. In the beginning, there was no man to cultivate the ground, so God held back until the right person came. In the meantime, God sent the mist (Genesis 2:4-6). I remember when I was a youth pastor, I would cry out in prayer that God should bring new members in! Until one day, He told me to quit praying that prayer! The state of the youth ministry at that time could not manage what we were asking for. So, God asked me to work on the leaders who will manage the souls coming. God did not allow the rain to fall because there were not enough people to work the ground.

To govern means to exercise dominion over a territory. Governance brings all the other system components together to create a perfect symphony. When God created the earth, He knew it could contain people and not only that, but he gave man the very ability to govern and have dominion over all creatures, and man took charge. There is much wisdom to draw from the system that God built! A story that inspires me to keep going is when I read how Moses managed the millions of people he led out of captivity and through the wilderness. An individual's ability to govern has nothing to do with age but everything to do with wisdom. Across all the aspects of wisdom systems, this is the most crucial. This is where the rubber hits the road, where the heavy lifting occurs, and where leadership and wisdom come into play. Governance ensures that everything is done consistently. When you put suitable systems in place, consistency is guaranteed.

The Parable of Talents

The parable of talents in Matthew 25:14-30 is a clear example that encapsulates the principle of governance. The master owned the resources, delegated them to his servants, knew what he entrusted, and came to ask for a report after some time. The master knew that he could not manage the talents himself but wanted them to multiply. The master had principles in place to ensure fairness in the distribution of the talents. The master expected the servants to yield returns even though he did not set expectations on the kind of return expected. Finally, this master gave the servants a timeframe for trading with the talents. While there are other principles to learn from this parable, it is also an example of what governance should look like.

Principles of Fairness

Principles are there to determine the modus operandi of a system. Principles must drive every system put in place. There must be limits to what you are willing to do and constraints on what you would never do as an individual or group. Principles will determine the unique aspects that promote fairness and equal opportunity in a system. For people not to be marginalized, a leader must enforce fairness and equality in the system they put in place.

It is the leader's responsibility to manage fairness within a system and to monitor its impact on the stakeholders within the same system. In discussing the fairness of a system, it is essential to note that it would be impossible to establish a system that fosters equality for a group or organization you do not belong to. Imagine a scenario where the desired goal is to build a system that supports and caters to the needs of women from minority ethnicities. If all the decision-makers are all men, there is no way one can guarantee equality. Fairness can be possible in any scenario if the principles used to determine the system's structure are accurately taken from the Bible and directly from God. Scripture-based principles are the best!

Why was God angry with David when he slept with Bathsheba? It was not because of his actions. God was displeased because of the unfairness of his actions towards Uriah, his servant. David took what belonged to someone else when God could have given him much more (2 Samuel 12:8). God punished David because he defiled the principle of fairness within the system he built. This was obvious when Nathan, the prophet, confronted him. The parable Nathan shared centred around the unfairness of the fictional king (2 Samuel 12:1-9), which was an indirect reference to David's actions. You would know the quality of wisdom a person is walking in by the depth of principles that they allow to govern them.

Arbitration & Remediation

Every system must make provision for arbitration or remediation. Every system will have elements who will intentionally or unintentionally attempt to trample on the rights of others in the system. It is not enough to have guiding principles without a governance system for arbitration, redress, or remedial action. In some cases, a governance system for arbitration, redress, or re-mediation provides clarity and an unbiased interpretation of the principles in cases where it is vague. The criticality of having an arbitration system was validated when God instituted one when putting the State of Israel together. God made provision for the priests to be judges. For a long time, Israel was primarily ruled by "judges" mainly because of the need to judge matters arising between inhabitants of the State of Israel. In Exodus 18, we see that Jethro gave Moses an administration system. Moses was to get the bylaws and constitution from God, while the sub-leaders were to ensure that the constitution was honoured and deviations unbiasedly addressed.

Building Blocks

Systems help to amplify the presence of wisdom in a person's life by adding virtue demonstrating knowledge and self-control (placing yourself under the constraint of principles). They build perseverance and habit training (to build a habit, you need endurance), bear the fruit of godliness (when people begin to see the nature of God manifest in you) and brotherly kindness (not comparing yourself to other people), and love.

But also for this very reason, giving all diligence, add to your faith virtue, to virtue knowledge, to knowledge self-control, to self-control perseverance, to perseverance godliness, to godliness brotherly kindness, and to brotherly kindness love. (2 Peter 1:5-7)

At the age of eight, Josiah governed a country filled with stubborn people. He led with excellence because he took advantage of the previous structure. The system amplified the wisdom he was already walking in as a young King. Credit can equally be given to the system and the wisdom of God upon David's life for King Josiah's success. Systems should be in place, so you're not there as a fish out of water. A righteous man can only get back up when the right system is in place for them.

Many of us can't display the wisdom of God because we lack a system in place. Many of the challenges we face can be solved by simply implementing a system.

Leadership Matters

Some countries have systems with the right tools, technologies and people but lack proper governance. It is often because of irresponsible leaders who foster waste and mismanagement of resources. It was different in Solomon's case, as he operated in divine wisdom. 2 Chronicles 2:17-18 outlines how Solomon built his palace; he first identified the critical tasks then found people to oversee each aspect. He understood that there needed to be a specific number of overseers to govern each task effectively.

Governance requires the right leader to be at the helm of affairs. Imagine these two scenarios and tell me which group you believe would be more successful. A group of dogs led by a lion, or a group of lions led by a dog. I firmly believe that the group of dogs led by a lion would be more successful. This is because eventually, the nature of the dogs would transform to that of their leader, the lion. People eventually grow up to become like their leaders.

Remember that the Bible tells us that Jesus Christ is the lion of the tribe of Judah, meaning that the more we follow His leading, the more we transform to become like Him. Because a system would always look like its leader, governance is the most critical piece in every system. John Maxwell once said that everything rises and falls on leadership. You might not have the right people, processes, or even technology but still, attain a semblance of success if blessed with the right leader. A wise leader will eventually raise great people who will develop the right processes and technology for success. Who leads you matters! May God make you a leader worth following in Jesus' Name!

The Principle of Delegation

No man can operate on this earth alone. Don't tell me you have a spouse; that doesn't count because they have become one! Therefore, you are still alone.

Intentional support systems and unintentional support systems

If you want to succeed consistently in something, you must put a support system in place. Even God understood the necessity of support systems. In establishing the five-fold ministries, he ensured that there were other systems of support for them all to lean on.

Moses had the people, process, and technology, but he didn't have the governance system in place for lasting success (Exodus 18). It took his father-in-law's correction for Moses to adjust. The process he was working with was not wise and was causing him to be stressed. Some people think they are okay because they can carry the burden until they move and realize they cannot do it. Jethro stepped in to correct Moses and helped him develop a more effective process. He gave Moses specific instructions on what system to follow.

He instructed Moses to appoint men who could do the work and fear God to assist him! The first requirement was that they feared God! People that spoke the truth and had integrity. Sometimes it's the people that are the problem. The people to be chosen to lead others had to hate covetousness! Jealousy is destructive and dangerous. The moment a jealous person notices something someone else has, they become envious. You would know from the way they look at the things you have. These men were chosen mainly according to their character, not ability. You would know someone has reached their capacity by the stress level they frequently experience.

Reporting

Nothing can be confirmed as completed until supervised, and someone sends in a report about it. Reporting should not only be used when reporting good things. Documenting the good, bad, and ugly reflects one's character. Everyone must have someone above them that they are accountable to. Even the top leader in a group should report to a group of people. As an individual, you might be more senior than everyone in your organization or group, but you are not more senior than everyone combined. Therefore a lead pastor can report to a church board. There is something about reporting to someone above us that keeps us on our toes. It is accountability, and in fact, this is one of the ways that I test character, that is, the fruit of the spirit. Reporting is good for you! It is dangerous not to report to anyone. I see many young people these days who do not have any reporting structure in place, to their own detriment. It is said that power corrupts, and absolute power corrupts absolutely.

Reporting something negative is not the end if you're under the right authority. David was always able to report his feelings. Essentially, he was telling God that this is my heart, I'm not here to pretend with you because you see it all. David never tried to hide anything from God. Ensure that your reporting structure is clear.

Avoid Waste

God made the earth, and then He put a man and woman in charge of it. When a system is established, someone must be charged to manage the system's resources to avoid waste. Proper governance helps to ensure that the resources provided are apportioned to meet each need. After Jesus fed the crowd of five thousand men, not including women and children, He told them to gather up the fragments. The system Jesus had in place included using the disciples as ushers, the baskets as a form of technology, and the seating arrangement in groups as the process. Evidence of proper governance is that little or nothing is wasted.

In Daniel chapter 6:1-3, King Darius realized that resources were not managed appropriately in his kingdom. As a result, he restructured the governance system in the kingdom by appointing 120 satraps over his many provinces, and he then appointed three leaders to oversee those satraps.

Governance in the Home

In the context of a home, God placed the man as head over his household to take responsibility and be accountable for those under his authority within the household. While under the husband's authority, the woman has the role of a wife. It is not true that every woman must submit to every man outside of marriage. The governance system that God established for a home is that once the man marries the woman, that woman comes under the husband's authority in their own home (Ephesians 5:22)! There are cases where a woman can legitimately be in authority over a man. This can happen in the church, workplace, community, and many other domains.

The governance system is there in the home, so children are covered and protected. Children are to be under the covering of their parents, not the other way around (Ephesians 6:1). Honour is a crucial aspect of this governance system, where a child consciously decides to honour their parent(s) regardless of what they do or don't do. The relationship between David and Saul is a perfect example of this. David and Saul weren't always in agreement with each other, and there was a point where Saul wanted to kill David. To protect himself, David had to distance himself from Saul. However, David still honoured Saul as a father in his heart, even from miles away. David understood the governance structure when it came to child/parent relationships. David knew that he needed to remain submitted under Saul's authority to remain under a spiritual covering (1 Samuel 24:11). David knew not to contemplate harming God's anointed one.

Governance in Unfriendly Territory

To continually succeed, you need to have the right perspective about enemies. Enemies are good when you have the proper system to counter their negative impact. When you know that people are waiting for you to fail, understand that they've prophesied your failure just by their desires. Make up your mind not to allow that demonic prophecy to come to pass.

The way we govern in a friendly environment must be different from how we govern in a hostile environment. Some governance techniques do not work out well mainly because there was not enough consideration for deliberate attempts to bring down the system. Nehemiah was one of such leaders who governed under a hostile environment, and there is a lot we can learn from him. In fact, in one instance, he asked his people to build with one hand while holding a sword in the other hand. How do you know when you are in a hostile environment? You know this when there are way more people wanting you to fail than those wanting you to succeed. Their thoughts, actions, and words against you are lethal weapons and must not be taken for granted. Do you know that if the people working in your system are exposed to discouraging words, it can reduce their productivity and motivation to work? A damaged motivation can eventually cause damage. You need to compensate for an oversupply of the things being attacked when building a governance system in such hostile environments.

In Nehemiah's example, they were surrounded by overwhelming discouragement. As such, Nehemiah deliberately and consciously over-motivated the people (Nehemiah 4:13). I can imagine Nehemiah charging the people every day and reminding them why they were doing what they were doing. Another thing that we saw Nehemiah do was to make provision for a sort of civil defence force. There are times when one must provide even physical protection to those in the system. To do that, you need to have a method for assessing the environment. These methods can be spiritual or physical using surveillance technology. Don't be naive into thinking that because you mean well, everyone means well.

Nehemiah was aware of the main enemies he had. There were mainly three people, namely Sanballat, Tobiah, and Geshem. When you find enemies that refuse to be disarmed after several attempts, you must understand that they have internal support from within your system. Nehemiah continuously faced stiff opposition until he finally realized the alliance that Tobiah had with Eliashib the high priest (Nehemiah 13:4-9). Remember, the friend of your enemy is your enemy. Whoever partners up with your enemy is your enemy. Jesus put it this way, "He who is not with Me is against Me, and he who does not gather with me scatters abroad" (Matthew 12:30).

Documentation of Guiding Principles

Guiding principles, rules, regulations, etc., must be documented in a constitution, bylaw or aptly named document to ensure fairness in a system. This document containing the principles guiding the distribution of resources within a system must be accessible and easily understandable by an entry-level member. A process for updating this document must also be in place to make sure that it represents current realities.

As the system matures, it will be expedient to have non-leadership members involved in updating the document that guides the system's affairs. Care must be taken to ensure that the group updating this document has the interest of only the system in mind. This guiding document is the source of authority for the operation of that system. Words form the basis for authority, and authority trumps power any day. The words contained in the governing documents are treated with utmost importance.

A system as small as a family or as large as a nation can and must operate within the context of the guiding principles document. The guiding principle documents should contain essential information. It should include specifics about all the points discussed in this governance chapter and other pertinent details.

CHAPTER 6

CHARACTERISTICS OF A HEALTHY SYSTEM

The human body comprises several systems, including the digestive, immune, and reproductive systems. The proper functioning of these systems helps ensure that we are healthy and strong. Each system I listed above has a unique way of notifying the rest of the body when there are issues with the health of that system. In the same way, there are specific signs we can look at to help us diagnose a system's health. There are also red flags that can alert us when a system is unhealthy or imbalanced. For example, you know your immune system is strong and vibrant when you recover quickly from cold or flu, have good gut health, and enjoy a sound sleep. But, the opposite is true when one's immune system is weak or compromised. Here we will explore traits of healthy systems beyond the human body.

Effectiveness

According to Merriam Webster's dictionary, effectiveness is the ability for something to do what it was created or intended to do. Effectiveness can be measured by consistent progress and goal accomplishment. A sound system has to be effective at achieving its goals. If the system in place does not reach the goals it ought to acquire, it is useless and should be replaced. Effectiveness ensures a system's primary purpose is accomplished continuously and consistently. Your loyalty should not be to a system, but to the result you anticipate. This approach of loyalty to the result and not the system will enable you to replace or repair an ill-functioning system when necessary.

A healthy system must keep its primary goals as the focus, however large the system becomes. This is where purposefulness comes into play. Purposefulness is a trait that a healthy system must keep at heart. The governance aspect of a system is responsible for ensuring the purpose of a system is adhered to. While efficiency is built into the people, processes, and technology, effectiveness is driven by the people and governance components of the system.

Efficiency

Merriam Webster's dictionary defines efficiency as producing desired results without wasting materials, time, or energy. The principle of efficiency redeems time, resources, and energy. Efficiency can apply to people, processes, technology, or governance approaches. When establishing a system's procedure, one must consider efficiency by ensuring that the people hired are enough to manage the system.

Can you imagine living in a country that does not have a traffic management system? It will lead to an unnecessary waste of time, energy, and other valuable resources that people could have used to generate value. A traffic system will make for the efficient use of the road network to ensure that people, goods, and services are transported efficiently. Likewise, any healthy system should ensure that all its parts flow easily and resources can get to where needed the most, as seamlessly as possible.

Fairness

Thriving within a system is as easy as following the system's dictates. This was one of the reasons for the early success of the American nation. America was founded on the idea of "The American Dream." There will always be those who will seek to manipulate the system to their advantage. Those in positions of authority must consider these things and provide tools for the oppressed to seek redress. Any system that will succeed and stand the test of time must not accommodate oppression or oppressors. Allowing the system to become like the Wild West will not encourage others to grow and advance within the system. As stated in the chapter on governance, a system that will last must have a process for interpreting, rewarding, and enforcing the guiding principles that the system abides by.

Systems that foster and support inequality and injustice will not last. As you can see in the world today, oppressed, and repressed people will always rise eventually and crush the unjust system. Modern examples of oppressed people pushing back are the Me Too movement, the Black Lives Matter movement, and the Arab Spring protests that saw many long-term leaders deposed. While no system other than that which is in heaven can be perfect, our job as apostles is to labour diligently to ensure that the needs of everyone who is a part of that system are catered to. Rewards and punishments must be clearly stated and enforced. It must be honoured when a reward is earned according to the system's parameters. When discipline is deserved, it must be served.

If mercy is extended in the place of judgement for one person, then the same approach must apply to everyone else within that system.

Love

A healthy system promotes love for every member of the system. You do not need to produce in a healthy system to be loved. Even though every member of the system should be encouraged to produce value to make the system better, the system must ensure that every member is loved and cared for at the barest minimum. A system that neglects its weak members will not stand the test of time. David echoed this idea when he and his men pursued after the invaders who took their wives, children, and property (1 Samuel 30:1-31). As the pursuit of the looters intensified, some of David's men were tired and could not continue the chase. While the soldiers who continued in the pursuit with David pressured him to ensure that those who could not continue did not share the spoils of war, David insisted they should. This decision was predicated on the principle of fairness. This principle underpins the need for a social network in every society. This principle encourages the elderly to receive care and support in their old age. It ensures that children are cared for and protected from abusers.

In most systems, you will find envious people. If envy is allowed to thrive in a system, there will be confusion and all kinds of evil things (James 3:16). A system where healthy competition, not destructive competition, is encouraged will be more productive for everyone. For example, the very nature of capitalism ensures the private ownership of capital, but that should not be at all cost. Rivalry and competition will lead to a system imploding. The system's leadership must ensure love and camaraderie while fostering healthy competition. Jacob's family was an example of an unhealthy system. Jacob followed in the father's footsteps, Isaac and openly favoured one child; as a result, Joseph was sold into slavery. Jesus also vehemently resisted every attempt by His disciples to be envious of one another. In one instance, James and John's mother came to Jesus asking Him to elevate her children at the expense of the other disciples but Jesus refused her request.

> Then the mother of Zebedee's sons came to Him with her sons, kneeling down and asking something from Him. And He said to her, "What do you wish?" She said to Him, "Grant that these two sons of mine may sit, one on Your right hand and the other on the left, in Your kingdom." But Jesus answered and said, "You do not know what you ask. Are you able to drink the cup that I am about to drink, and be baptized with the baptism that I am baptized with?" They said to Him, "We are able." So He said to them, "You will indeed drink My cup, and be baptized with the baptism that I am baptized with, but to sit on My right hand and on My left is not Mine to give, but it is for those for whom it is prepared by My Father." And when the ten heard it, they were greatly displeased with the two brothers. But Jesus called them to Himself and said, "You know that the rulers of the Gentiles lord it over them, and those who are great exercise authority over them. Yet it shall not be so among you; but whoever desires to become great among you, let him be your servant. And whoever desires to be first among you, let him be your slave— just as the Son of Man did not come to be served, but to serve, and to give His life a ransom for many." (Matthew 20:20-28)

This bizarre request angered the remaining disciples because it attempted to introduce uncertainty to Jesus' governance system. Promotion should be by merit and not favouritism, nepotism, tribalism, or partisanship.

Leaders must never show favouritism to others. There will always be those who will violate the integrity of a system and bring shame to it. While those who dishonour the system should be penalized, everyone must know that they have equal chances at enjoying the privileges made available by the system. Ensure that while your system does not tolerate violations of its principles, the violators are penalized with love. Have you thought about why a criminal whose life is in danger must still be protected by law enforcement officers, irrespective of their offence? Have you thought about why prisoners of war must still be cared for, regardless of their crimes? Love is what it takes to keep a system together because love never fails (1 Corinthians 13:8). You cannot use hate to build a loving system. The oppressed will always turn around to destroy the system of oppression. Promote the flow of love from all parts of your system to another. Avoid silos and any attempt to foster division within your system.

One of the pieces of evidence of love within a system is collaboration. Psalms 133 speaks about the blessings from unity within a system. It is good to dwell together in harmony. Unity will trigger the flow of anointing for supernatural results and promote collaboration within your system. Encourage everyone to relate with one another and forgive intentional and unintentional hurt. Since it is practically impossible for people to dwell together without stepping on each other's toes, every system must learn to practice forgiveness. Forgiveness is the art of letting go of an offence and giving offenders a second chance. Forgiveness takes place when a person or people decide to extend love instead of responding with hatred. While there is a place for punishment and justice for offenders, one should avoid grudges and offence. Unfortunately, phrases like "lest we forget" and "we will never forgive" have become famous rallying cries issued by countries' leaders in response to atrocities committed against them. Build systems filled with love and watch them grow beyond your imagination.

Peace

Another defining characteristic of a healthy system is peace. Peace is evidence that all the system parts are functioning as designed. Peace is the absence of anxiety and stress. Rest is only possible when there is peace. When peace reigns in the human body, it is because the body is void of pain, stress, and agony. The same applies to a system, like a family, organization, or even a nation. As the excellence within a system grows, the peace within it will grow. Since peace is dependent on excellence within a system, and excellence is dependent on wisdom, it means that wisdom is the critical ingredient for peace within a system. That wisdom is needed for peace to reign within a system is not a surprise. The reign of King Solomon was described as one of the most peaceful for the nation of Israel.

> *For he ruled over all the region on this side of the River from Tiphsah even to Gaza and had peace on all sides. During Solomon's lifetime Judah and Isreal, from Dan to Beersheba, lived in safety, everyone under their own vine and under their own fig tree.* (1 Kings 4:24-25).

Additionally, we see a clear correlation between the wisdom Solomon enjoyed and the peace he enjoyed.

> *So the Lord gave Solomon wisdom, as He had promised him; and there was peace between Hiram and Solomon, and the two of them made a treaty together* (I Kings 5:12).

Peace is not a result of the absence of enemies but the result of the display of wisdom. A system that has all its bases covered will operate peacefully. For example, for peace to reign in a home, the critical elements that cause conflict must be addressed systematically. Discussions about communication, financial administration, effective and efficient task distribution, guiding principles, in-law and friendship management, future planning and goals, spiritual enlightenment, etc., should be had and decisions documented and implemented. When you pray for peace, you should expect wisdom to organize affairs for lasting peace. Proverbs 3:17 corroborates that there is peace and pleasantness where there is wisdom.

Some people sadly do not like peace because it seems boring. They fail to understand that there cannot be growth without peace, and without growth, the system will eventually die. Peace is needed for productivity. Peace is required for creativity. Peace is necessary for clarity and so on. No wonder Romans 12:18 and Hebrews 12:14 both repeat the instruction to pursue peace as much as possible. However, the reality is that in some cases, it takes war to secure peace. Remember that Jesus confirmed that He had given us His peace.

> *Peace I leave with you, My peace I give to you; not as the world gives do I give to you. Let not your heart be troubled, neither let it be afraid* (John 14:27).

For every troubled person reading this book, may the God of all peace fill your heart, mind, and body with His peace now in Jesus' name.

Abundance

We understand from science that the body thrives when it is at peace. Peace will lead to creativity, clarity, and eventually productivity. Another evidence of a healthy system is abundance or increase. The reign of King Solomon was marked with unprecedented abundance. As a result of the rest Israel enjoyed, they could focus on increasing their devotion to God.

> *But now the Lord my God has given me rest on every side; there is neither adversary nor evil occurrence. And behold, I*

propose to build a house for the name of the Lord my God, as the Lord spoke to my father David, saying, "Your son, whom I will set on your throne in your place, he shall build the house for My Name." (1 Kings 5:4-5).

Beloved, until there is peace, there cannot be abundance. Solomon was able to focus on building the house of the Lord because there was peace on every side. When a person is labelled as mentally unstable, it means they lack peace of mind. Abundance is assured in a system when every component plays its part. The Bible teaches that two are better than one because they will generate more results if they work as one (Ecclesiastes 4:9). The power of synergy comes into play in a healthy system. Synergy occurs when the whole is greater than the sum of its parts. Where there is synergy, there is exponential multiplication, not addition. Normally, one plus one equals two, but when synergy comes into play, one plus one can be anything from two to infinity. This power of synergy is designed to work powerfully in a united environment. Someone once said that order would automatically create an increase. A healthy system will enforce order, and this order will in turn lead to abundance.

One of the most prosperous countries in the world is Switzerland. The Swiss are known not only for their chocolate and watches but also for their wealth. As of the time of writing this book, Switzerland is one of the wealthiest nations in the world on a per capita income basis. Many countries and wealthy individuals keep their wealth in Switzerland mainly because of integrity and peace. The Swiss have put a system in place to ensure the integrity of financial transactions, which has earned them the reputation of being a financial haven.

Joy

Joy is one of many ingredients that go into a healthy system. Joy is also an output to expect from a healthy system. A healthy system will be a joyful system. Psalms 2:4 records that God laughs in heaven. The system in heaven is filled with so much joy. A joy-filled marriage is a healthy marriage, bearing the fruit of joy. A joy-filled family is a healthy family bearing the fruit of joy. Joy is needed in every system for it to be fruitful. To emphasize the significance of joy in every system, you will agree that every nation and culture provides entertainment. Every single culture or nation on the face of the earth has incorporated joy as part of its culture. If your system is void of joy, it will soon become a graveyard.

CHAPTER 7

FIREWALLING THE SYSTEM

Every system must be well guarded and protected from assaults from within and without. From the beginning of time, attempts have been made to either destroy systems or compromise them. When you study history, you will find that the early years in the formation of nations were when they experienced the most intense attacks. In recent history, the construction of the Israeli state is an example to learn from. Modern-day Israel was formed May 14th, 1948, and that same year; five Arab nations invaded this newly formed nation. Israel triumphed in that battle because it was prepared for it. David Ben Gurion, the first Israeli Prime Minister drilled into the psyche of the newly formed nation to expect war and indeed war came.

Solomon, the newly minted king of Israel, had a brother named Adonijah. Adonijah was the man who attempted to usurp his father, King David's throne. When his plan failed and Solomon successfully became king, Adonijah made a strange request. In 1 Kings 2:13, Adonijah went to King Solomon's mother, reminding her that Solomon's kingdom was meant to be his. What an audacious statement! Adonijah also told King Solomon's mother to ask Solomon for Abishag the Shunammite as his wife. You would remember that this was the same lady that king David's aides brought to him to keep him warm during his old age. I'm sure you might be wondering why Adonijah made such a request. Better still, Solomon's response might be even more shocking if you don't understand the implication of Adonijah's request. Immediately Solomon heard the request; he determined that Adonijah must be executed. I always wondered why Solomon took such a drastic step and why he did not just deny the request and correct his brother? Solomon was determined to protect the new kingdom (the new system) from compromise. He knew that if he granted the request for Abishag, more demands would eventually weaken the kingdom. We can draw several rules for protecting a system from internal and external attacks from this story.

Rule Number 1: Delegate wisely.

Once power and authority have been given away, it will be challenging to take them back. The enemy's plot to kill, steal and destroy started with Adam and Eve (Genesis 3). However, amid the enemy's deception, God's plan for redeeming His people back to Himself also took flight. Jesus, the hope of the world, was called into the picture 2,000 years later to take back all power and authority. As you can see from Genesis chapter 3, it was easy for a man to forfeit their God-given authority. Yet it took over two millennia before that authority could be restored through Christ. Authority can be easily given but difficult to take back. Adam and Eve were given dominion over the earth, but they blindly traded their dominion through a piece of fruit. To avoid further damage, God immediately chased Adam and Eve out of the Garden of Eden to avoid eating from the tree of eternal life. God knew that if Adam and Eve ate from the tree of eternal life, another repetition of satan's rebellion would occur. What valuable thing have you forfeited because you delegated prematurely?

The Bible tells us in Exodus chapter 18 of how Moses graduated into servant leadership. Before Exodus chapter 18, Moses had already been on a very long journey with the children of Israel. Moses nearly destroyed himself and those he led because he wanted to do everything independently. Most of Moses' leadership journey was filled with long, hot days of frustration. The burden of millions of people was on the shoulders of one man. But, at the very beginning of Exodus 18, we saw things take a different turn for Moses. Busy with his usual duties and responsibilities, Moses was confronted by his father-in-law, Jethro, who carefully observed how Moses managed the needs of the people. Jethro looked at Moses that day and shook his head, and said, "young man, if you continue like this, you will kill yourself. You and the people will continue to be frustrated because of your poor leadership". Thank God for authority figures that aren't afraid to correct and speak the truth when needed! Jethro corrected Moses and provided direction on how his leadership should be restructured, ensuring that the load and responsibility were shared amongst able men. Men that fear God, men that are truthful and hate covetousness. Authority for leadership was given to these men because they had the capacity to handle the responsibility it came with. Moses humbly accepted this advice, which demonstrated selflessness. He realized that to be an excellent example of leadership for the people, he had to show love by sharing the responsibility of leadership.

Rule 2: No Exceptions

Exceptions are one of the cheapest ways to weaken a system. The moment you begin to grant exceptions, keep in mind that everyone would want them, and now there is no more need for

INTERCONNECTED SYSTEMS

a system. Giving exceptions is dangerous because it also shows that the person granting them does not believe in the system's ability to perform. Think about it; you want people to know that following the system will guarantee their success. That is why granting exceptions would work against your ability to convince others to follow the system. You might be thinking, "how about scenarios where the system in place would make a simple task complicated?". I don't consider those as exceptions. Instead of granting an exception, simply view it as an opportunity for setting up a different system for those circumstances. For example, suppose you have decided to put a system in place for meetings. In that case, you want to ensure that people who require extended conversations follow the process of setting up an appointment for those conversations.

On the other hand, there are times when the system is working as designed, but some people don't want to follow the system, perhaps because they think they are above the system or they don't see a need for it in the first place. This is prevalent among family members, friends, and people that have been present before the system was implemented. If you think about it deeper, this is really what the children of Israel struggled with when they came out of Egypt, which eventually led to the death of an entire generation in the wilderness. God, through Moses, was trying to put them in a system that would guarantee their survival and prosperity as a nation. Even though it was an excruciating task to enforce a system, it had immense benefits. Change is one of the most difficult things to adjust to, even when it would benefit them. Additionally, others would be more inclined to follow the systems if they see those close to the leader following and honouring the system. When managing a system like this, it is essential to note that exceptions can work against your ability to solidify the system.

When God the Father sent Jesus to the earth, he had to follow the system He put in place. Jesus had to be born of a woman; he grew as a human being and was eventually baptized like everyone else. A leader should help people around them understand that seeking to circumvent the system is a sign of dishonour. If you genuinely honour a person, you will show respect to them and the product of their thinking which includes the process they put in place. A leader must also ensure that they follow the system they put in place. There are cases where a system is put in place to manage expenses, but the one leading does something different. By doing this, you are encouraging others to do the same thing. So, if you're asking people to submit receipts and follow a process to get reimbursed, you must also do the same and make this process straightforward. I came across an article that showed the CEO of Tesla, Elon Musk, lining up to charge his vehicle in one of their public charging stations like everyone else. Can you imagine the impression that this would leave on an average person? As a leader, you must lead by example. Here at Cornerstone, I am bound by the systems that manage our finances and other aspects of the ministry. When it gets to a point when it is not feasible for me to personally follow certain processes, it is my responsibility to make sure that those acting on my behalf do so.

Rule 3: No Favouritism

Some systems are designed only to work for certain groups in a population. This is the epitome of systemic racism. When a system is not fair, it is set up to favour certain people. In such situations, that system will not last. It is sometimes difficult to realize that your system only favours a select few. The best way to avoid building a system that only favours a specific group is to get a broad representation of people involved in developing the system. It is difficult to consider the needs of physically disabled people if all the people involved in developing the transportation system are physically able. This perspective is critical because we sometimes assume that a biased system was intentionally designed as such. Bias in a system can be the result of an honest mistake. It will shock you how much God considered and factored into the laws he gave to the children of Israel. He designed the laws to benefit them and created each law with citizens, refugees, and immigrants in mind.

Rule 4: Know When to Tweak the System

There are times when a system that has been built must be revised. Do you know how many amendments the US constitution contains? How about the constitution of the country you are from? You can never cover all your bases on the first try, no matter how much you try. There is a story in the Bible about a group of sisters who lost their father. According to the laws of Moses, they were not going to have access to their father's inheritance because they had no brothers (Numbers 27:1-11). Remember that this law was handed down to them by God Himself. Instead of accepting this verdict, these ladies pleaded their case to God through Moses. The same God that delivered the law revised it to suit the ladies. God Himself knew when the law that He made had to be adjusted. As a matter of principle, you must set time aside to revise the system at predetermined times. This can be on a yearly, quarterly, monthly basis. We must be very careful not to become custodians of past traditions to protect a system. You will notice that even though Coca-Cola has changed the Coke bottle's exterior presentation over the years, content has remained the same.

When do you know that a system needs to be tweaked? A system is due for revision when it is no longer adding the intended value. Another indication could also be when the system becomes more of a burden to bear than a blessing to enjoy. When valid complaints about the system continue to outweigh the testimonies from the system, you'll realize that it is time to return to the drawing board.

Rule 5: Know When to Overhaul the System Completely

In the beginning, we understand that God made the heavens and the earth and humankind. We also know that the devil came and usurped man's authority in the garden of Eden which led to Adam and Eve being kicked out. Until the last prophet in the Old Testament, God attempted to restore man based on the law. However, it got to a point where God realized that his approach needed to change; this decision heralded the plan of redemption through Christ. Jesus said that He did not come to abolish the law but fulfill it. In other words, he came to bring about a new system, that is, the New Testament. In this new system, slaughtering animals is no longer a requirement for restoration. Instead, faith in Jesus Christ has become the new requirement of the propitiation of sin.

The moment you realize that the system cannot continually satisfy the reason for its existence, it is most likely time for it to be overhauled. As a leader, you must ensure that you are not over-attached to the system no matter how effective it is. It would be best to be attached to the system's goals but not the system delivering them. Systems usually have a shelf life, and we must know the expiry date. There is a limit to how often you can patch a cloth, and a time will come when the fabric itself will have to be replaced. Jesus clearly said that man was not made for the law, but the law was made for man (Mark 2:27).

As it relates to Christendom, it is imperative to understand that there are times when systems must be overhauled. I have watched in dismay how ministries grow to a point where the adults call

all the shots without giving room for the younger generation to assume leadership roles. The issue is often that the adults take on the role of custodians of tradition. One way or the other, they mistake the message of Christ as being the same as the method for communicating the message. Throughout history, practices have changed, but in true bible-believing churches, the message has remained the same: that message is that Jesus Christ is Lord. The Bible tells us that Samson fought a battle with the jawbone of an ass (Judges 15:16). But, the fantastic thing is that after he won the battle, he threw away the very tool he used to win that particular fight. Specific systems are limited to a geographical region, while some are limited to a particular demographic. We must understand this so that we are not forcing a system that has worked in one place into another where it is doomed to fail.

Rule 6: Out with the Old; In with the New

There is a reason why the Bible advises us not to pour new wine into old wineskins (Matthew 9:14-17). It is to ensure that new content is put in a new container. God cannot put a fresh anointing in an old character or mindset. This same concept applies in a secular setting. When leaders take on a new position, they must adjust their supporting leadership team. People who do not understand this often assume it is done to secure loyalty. These practices have scriptural backing (Luke 5:33-39) because the best way to destroy a thing is from within. People whose sole target is to attack and resist progress from within must be quickly identified. They may stand with you, pretend to be on your side but are nowhere close to being on your side. Beware of such wolves in sheepskin! God Himself told Joshua to follow what He told Moses to do when they arrived in the promised land.

> *Now the Lord spoke to Moses in the plains of Moab by the Jordan, across from Jericho, saying, "Speak to the children of*

Israel, and say to them: 'When you have crossed the Jordan into the land of Canaan, then you shall drive out all the inhabitants of the land from before you, destroy all their engraved stones, destroy all their moulded images, and demolish all their high places; you shall dispossess the inhabitants of the land and dwell in it, for I have given you the land to possess. And you shall divide the land by lot as an inheritance among your families; to the larger, you shall give a larger inheritance, and to the smaller, you shall give a smaller inheritance; there everyone's inheritance shall be whatever falls to him by lot. You shall inherit according to the tribes of your fathers. But if you do not drive out the inhabitants of the land from before you, then it shall be that those whom you let remain shall be irritants in your eyes and thorns in your sides, and they shall harass you in the land where you dwell. Moreover, it shall be that I will do to you as I thought to do to them.' (Numbers 33:50-56)

Joshua followed those instructions and destroyed everything that was pre-existing. He destroyed the stones, which served as landmarks and reminders of the past system. God intended for them to destroy the previous system entirely and start fresh. Suppose you allow the old system to stay. Allowing remnants from a previous system will cause the eventual destruction of the new system.

Rule 7: Immediately you take territory, establish a new system

Immediately territories are taken, the next step is to establish systems. God made the heavens and the earth and immediately set up a system for the way things should work in the newly created territory. God led the children of Israel from Egypt to Canaan land, but before they set foot in the land promised to them,

INTERCONNECTED SYSTEMS

God gave clear direction on systems to implement to secure their establishment (Deuteronomy 12:1-26). In adopting a new way of life, the Israelites learnt how to fight, raise families, and build lasting structures. Remember that you cannot get better results than your predecessor if you follow the same system your predecessor followed. Remember that the secret to the stability of anything is the system backing it up. Invest your time and energy into establishing and sustaining a lasting system, and you will not regret it. A system is the greatest miracle you can ever ask for from God. Have you ever imagined whether miracles happen in heaven? Of course not! Miracles do not need to happen in heaven because everything operates under a perfect system.

HOW TO THRIVE IN A SYSTEM

Not everyone will realistically have the power to effect change to a system immediately. People operating in an apostolic capacity or those that possess apostolic giftings are primarily responsible for designing and implementing systems.

You can still thrive in a system not built with you in mind. The key to lasting success and promotion in such a system is understanding. Study the system so much that you begin to see how it can work for you and cater to your needs. There are many systems today that were established without minority populations in mind. Yet, we still see and hear of countless success stories of individuals thriving and making a worldwide impact despite the discrimination in the system they live in. If you find yourself in a system where change seems like a far-fetched idea and are overcome with frustration, do not be discouraged! Settle down and begin to analyze the different aspects that make up that system closely. There is a solution and hope for change, and that change is you. You can thrive within any system and eventually bring about positive change.

INTERCONNECTED SYSTEMS

While some systems can be changed incrementally (evolution), some must be blown away and replaced (revolution). Either way, you cannot bring about change to a system that you don't understand. You also cannot change a system that you don't honour. If you're among the category of disenfranchised or marginalized people, be of good cheer because you will be armed with weapons that will wipe out your frustration and feeling of helplessness and hopelessness. How was it that a person like Abigail could thrive in a marriage with an unwise man like Nabal (1 Samuel 25), while someone like Michal was unable to succeed in the house of a man after God's own heart (King David)? How can you thrive in a system that you did not build or that was not built for you?

Take Time to Understand the System

I watch in amazement sometimes how a person can step into a place for the first time and attempt to fix problems they do not understand. This embarrassing mistake is because it never occurred to them that they should study the system first. Without adequate background knowledge and information, you run the risk of repeating past mistakes or running into even more significant challenges. Many countries that "deposed" autocratic rulers end up with even more autocratic leaders. Examples are Cuba, Venezuela, Russia, etc.

Every system has a constitution, a manifesto, or a document explaining how the system operates. Locate those documents and study them enough to understand the ins and outs of where you currently find yourself. Remember, you cannot dominate what you don't understand. Understanding a system can seem like an uphill task, especially if the system has been in operation for a long time. Here are a few thoughts to keep in mind as you set your mind on understanding the system you are in:

- I must understand the system before I can bring change to it.
- No system is impossible to change, no matter how unfair and wicked it is.
- I must honour the system before I can be rewarded by it.
- No matter how evil or corrupt the system is, I must never be a part of any rebellion against it. (1 Samuel 15:23)

The Bible provides many examples of characters who successfully thrived in wicked systems. Joseph, Esther, and Daniel are examples to follow! They show us that we don't have to become corrupt to change a corrupt system. Hate cannot cast away hate; anger cannot overcome anger. Love is the only virtue powerful enough to overcome all forms of negative resistance. Joseph's life is the perfect example to learn this concept from. The common saying goes, "if you cannot beat them, join them." I want to challenge you by changing that to "if you cannot beat them, keep loving them until they join you." I love the saying "where there is a will, there is a way"! The spirit of boldness is upon you to positively change that complex system you find yourself in. Here are a few ways to understand any system.

Observation

The objective of a spy is to observe and gather intelligence carefully. To observe is to give active attention to a thing. Thorough observation requires a certain level of curiosity and sensitivity to detail, both obvious and hidden. You can say that spies are professional observers. Their job is not to pay attention to every detail but to the salient details. To observe something carefully is to see what others would not usually notice. In Joshua chapter 2:1, Joshua refrained from sending the Israeli military to invade Jericho because he saw it fit to first send spies to gather intelligence. The spies encountered Rehab, the prostitute. In another instance, God Himself instructed the Israelites to spy on a land before invading it.

> *And the Lord spoke to Moses, saying, "Send men to spy out the land of Canaan, which I am giving to the children of Israel; from each tribe of their fathers, you shall send a man, everyone a leader among them."* (Numbers 13:1-3)

Observation is most effective when done with our eyes and our heart (Proverbs 23:26). Observation through the eyes and heart will help you capture the spirit behind a system. A targeted study (as we will examine shortly) will help you capture the system's written principles. In capturing the spirit behind a system, the eyes are used to see, while the heart meditates on the "why" (Philippians 4:8-9). No matter how much we look with our natural eyes, unless revelation is released, we cannot observe any actionable information (Luke 10:23-24).

Mentorship

For an observation to be beneficial in understanding a system, it must be focused on the key individuals within that organization. My advice is to locate those key individuals and initiate a mentorship relationship. One cannot be exposed to specific details until they connect with the right person in a mentorship relationship. Privileged information is often shared in such relationships. In cases where critical information is discerned, the correct application can only be shared when there is a deep connection between the mentor and mentee. This is where the mentor would guide specific steps as they begin to navigate through a system. A mentor will help you see the proper steps to move to the next level. Many people struggle to submit to mentorship. Some fear rejection, while some are proud. They avoid it because they either believe they are unworthy or too good for mentorship.

A trained eye can quickly identify a person's struggle. The most outstanding mentor is the Holy Spirit because he not only answers questions and provides direction, but He challenges you in your thinking and choices.

An example of joining by the hip mentorship is the story leading up to Elijah's ascension to heaven in II Kings 2:7-14.

> *And fifty men of the sons of the prophets went and stood facing them at a distance, while the two of them stood by the Jordan. Now Elijah took his mantle, rolled it up, and struck the water; and it was divided this way and that so that the two of them crossed over on the dry ground. And so it was when they had crossed over, that Elijah said to Elisha, "Ask! What may I do for you, before I am taken away from you?" Elisha said, "Please let a double portion of your spirit be upon me." So he said, "You have asked a hard thing. Nevertheless, if you see me when I am taken from you, it shall be so for you; but if not, it shall not be so." Then it happened, as they continued on and talked, that suddenly a chariot of fire appeared with horses of fire and separated the two of them; and Elijah went up by a whirlwind into heaven. And Elisha saw it, and he cried out, "My father, my father, the chariot of Israel and its horsemen!" So he saw him no more. And he took hold of his own clothes and tore them into two pieces. He also took up the mantle of Elijah that had fallen from him and went back and stood by the bank of the Jordan. Then he took the mantle of Elijah that had fallen from him, and struck the water, and said, "Where is the Lord God of Elijah?" And when he also had struck the water, it was divided this way and that; and Elisha crossed over.*

Elisha, alongside the other fifty spiritual sons of Elijah, the prophet, knew that Elijah was going to be taken up by God. Only Elisha, however, was able to observe the timing of this information and thus benefit from it. We saw a similar occurrence in

Jesus' ministry as well. Jesus said the secret behind His exploits in ministry was to observe the Father and repeat what He saw the Father do (John 5:19-20). Friends, there is much to gain from mentorship, especially when there is a deep love connection between you and the one you are observing and learning from. One of the benefits of mentorship or being under spiritual authority is the privilege of seeing the mentor's success system up close.

Targeted Study

Systems can be understood by studying documents that outline the makeup and structure of the system. The purpose of a targeted study is to seek out uncommon and sometimes classified information that can only be found in the blueprint manual of a system. The fantastic thing about understanding a system through its foundational documents is that it gives backdoor access to information on how to reap the most benefit from that system. If a person works for a company that offers bonuses and promotes employees often, but for whatever reason, has never received any such thing after ten years of exceptional work, I recommend that this individual stop and ask questions. If nothing seems to change, I will urge them to search for specific work promotion policies to use as the basis for challenging the system. If your situation ever calls for a targeted approach, ensure that you thoroughly read the documents you come across to understand the rationale behind them before taking steps. Some examples of different founding documents are the Bible, union policies, by-laws, constitutions.

Daniel and his friends thrived in a system not built for their rising (Daniel 1:3-21). Why? Because they took his time to study Babylonian culture. With the help of God on his side, Daniel was able to distinguish himself and benefit from a system that was meant to defile him and everything he believed in. Daniel became more excellent than his colleagues without engaging in anything undignifying. Friend, there is great hope for you despite what you may be up against! Before you allow yourself to criticize a system, discipline yourself first to study it (2 Timothy 2:15).

From Daniel's example, we now know that a targeted study can also be specific to a person or group of people that designed the system. Hidden in every system are perks intended to benefit those that created the system. Those hidden benefits are called backdoors. In software programming, a backdoor is typically known to the programmer only and often involves shortcuts to benefit from the software application. Backdoors hidden in the education system can only be identified when studying those who created the system and their intentions. Backdoors in real estate can only be located by understanding the identity and motivations of those who developed the system.

There is no learning without questions. A study can only be beneficial when you have genuine questions that require answers. Do you remember when Jesus stayed back in the temple without His parents' knowledge? Jesus was found in the temple listening to those teaching the word of God and then asking questions.

> *Now, so it was that after three days they found Him in the temple, sitting in the midst of the teachers, both listening to them and asking them questions. And all who heard Him were astonished at His understanding and answers. So, when they saw Him, they were amazed; and His mother said to Him, "Son, why have You done this to us? Look, your father and I have sought You anxiously."* (Luke 2:46-48).

You can never understand or benefit from something you won't first observe, intentionally study, and question. I mentioned earlier that in carrying out a targeted study, one must first ask genuine questions you need answers to, before taking steps. Without humility, you will not ask honest pertinent questions. Humble yourself to listen or observe and boldly ask questions before, during and after your study with the desire to be enlightened. Remember that your goal is to understand the system you have found yourself in, not to prove how smart you are.

A story in the Old Testament illustrates that any system can be changed when understood. An interesting case was brought into Moses' courtroom in Numbers 27:1-11. After the loss of their father, a group of women, known as the daughters of Zelophehad, approached Moses and the Elders seeking genuine answers for their current dilemma. These women approached Moses and the elders humbly. Even though their situation seemed unfortunate, I believe they understood that if they were to secure anything close to an inheritance, their approach to the current system needed to be adequately measured in humility and wisdom. From the way they pleaded their case, you can tell that they had a thorough understanding of the current system, but still, there were gaps in their knowledge. Hence why they needed clarification and a solution. There is no system that God cannot change when we approach it with a genuine heart first to understand! Remember all power and authority in heaven and on earth has been given to Christ!

Until you understand what makes up a system, you cannot influence change into it. To change a system that is not working for you, study it. Then, make your demands, and boldly take steps to state your case before the decision-makers.

Prayer

Often, the enemy will limit a person's understanding to keep them bound in an unideal system. Systems that have spiritual signatures can only be understood through prayer. Prayer would help to attack and break through any hindrance to our understanding of that system. Daniel shows us the power of engaging in prayer to understand the system that oppressed the Israelites and kept them in slavery (Daniel 9). Daniel did not receive the revelation he needed until he began fasting and praying. The moment he engaged these warfare weapons, the answer to his request was released. But the enemy carried out his regular duties by sending a demonic personality to resist and delay the revelation that God sent Daniel. The Bible identified this personality as the prince and king of Persia. In Jeremiah 33:3, we see that we cannot see great and mighty things until we call on God in prayer. Some prevailing systems will remain an enigma until we cry out to God in prayer.

Generational curses are systems by demonic entities to keep a group of people bound. The longer a curse remains, the more aligned the culture of that group of people will be to the demonic system. But I believe that the same God that gave Daniel revelation of the diabolical system the enemy was using to keep the Israelites down will open your understanding to any generational force holding your family down.

Like the story of the persistent widow and the unjust judge, continue to be relentless in making your desire for understanding known to God in the place of prayer (Luke 18:1-8)! The answer will come speedily, In Jesus' name! The Bible says that in all our getting, we should get understanding (Proverbs 4:7). It takes the inspiration of the Holy Ghost for us to gain understanding. Have you ever sat to read something and read it over several times and still not understand it? Most likely, it is because you have not involved the Holy Ghost in your search for understanding. Involve Him, do not give up on your quest for understanding and you will be glad you did not. Persistence is a trait territory takers must-have. Until we know systems within a territory and have the ability and authority to change them, we have not yet conquered that territory.

DEMONIC SYSTEMS

The enemy is always after God's children, working tirelessly to kill, steal, and destroy good things in their lives. He has many systems in place to accomplish his goals. In 2 Corinthians 2:11, the bible lists what some of the devices and systems are that the enemy specializes in manipulating. He causes people to be afflicted and manipulates government systems and processes to hinder the progress of God's children. Therefore, when I counsel people, I ask the Holy Spirit for help to identify the root cause of the issue. The Holy Spirit has often helped realize the root cause of many people's pain, problems, and suffering dating back to their upbringing, aka "childhood trauma." Until we can identify these areas, we will continue to fall prey to the enemy's wiles.

Instruments of Demonic Control
Pain
The Bible shares with us a tragic story in Genesis 35:16 of the enemy's attempt to turn a blessing into a curse. In deep pain

resulting from childbirth, Rachel was demonically influenced to name her son Ben-oni, reflecting the pain and suffering she endured. The enemy knows the power in a name given by an authority figure. Had Jacob not been sensitive to the enemy's scheme, their child would have grown up to manifest the name initially given to him by Rachel. Jacob understood and made a timely and wise decision by changing the name from Ben-oni to Benjamin. Oh, what a difference a name can make.

Pain is an instrument of control. We see this even when it comes to emotional and psychological pain. When a person is emotionally hurt and is bombarded with difficult memories, there are times when they resort to self-destructive coping mechanisms such as drugs or alcohol to self-soothe. These destructive coping mechanisms are what the enemy hopes for when he inflicts people with pain. It indirectly leads a person down a path that leads to utter destruction.

Shame

Shame is one of the filthy garments the enemy tries to clothe blood-washed Christians with. Although unjustified, Judas' betrayal of Jesus caused him great shame. As a result, he eventually hung himself. The enemy's evil plan with shame is to make a person so disappointed and disgusted with themselves that they refuse any extension of love, mercy, or forgiveness. The devil will convince them that judgement is the only way to redeem themselves. You see, the voice of shame is always asking, "how could I have done this," but the question you should ask yourself instead is, "how could I have not done it?" What is it that you have done that is still haunting you? What is the unpardonable sin that you believe God cannot forgive you for? Beloved, you are an imperfect being in the process of perfection through Christ. Understand that you are still a work in progress.

When you hear that someone committed suicide, often, it is because of shame. Shame is a potent weapon of control the enemy uses. It has the power to make a small thing big and a "big" thing bigger. Sometimes all you must do is laugh at yourself. I've been in situations where I stood up to speak, but I could not even say a word because of how afraid I was. The enemy tried to use this as a stronghold, but I quickly learned to strike back at the enemy. Laughing at yourself is strategy comedians often use. When the enemy reminds you of something you've done wrong, laugh! It's good for the soul. There are some that the enemy has clothed with shame from open correction or traumatic experiences. He is desperate and will use anything to inflict shame to leave a person questioning their worthiness. In Mark 14;72, Peter immediately became ashamed after denying Christ. Thankfully Christ quickly restored him because He still had a plan and purpose for him. Even when Peter questioned his worth, Christ still wanted him (John 21:15-19). You may have discounted yourself as unusable because of your past mistakes, but God still says He still wants to use you.

Guilt & Condemnation

This tool is what the enemy uses to make people feel as though they are not in right standing with God. If not for condemnation, many of us would be operating in confidence the Bible speaks of in Proverbs 30:30. But, the truth is that the word of God says that "There is therefore now no condemnation to those who are in Christ Jesus, who do not walk according to the flesh, but according to the Spirit." (Romans 8:1-2).

No matter the sin, go to God in prayer. Even if you believe you have committed the unpardonable sin, let God be the one to tell you that, instead of the devil or his human agents.

Condemnation is tied to the hip with judgment, which declares a life sentence of punishment for anyone who sins. However, conviction corrects with the right hand and extends mercy and grace with the left, so a person is not left to the destruction of sin or condemnation. The woman caught in adultery in John chapter 8:2-11 was on her way to being condemned until Jesus stepped in to extend mercy and grace! Do you know that sometimes you can feel blamed for something that is not your fault? You cannot imagine how many children are carrying the weight of their parents' mistakes from a failed marriage, or remaining in an abusive relationship, convinced that it is punishment for previous errors.

When guilt and condemnation come knocking on your door, admit your wrong immediately and ask God or the human being who was wronged for mercy. Mercy has been designed in such a way that whoever genuinely asks for it must get it. If Jesus can heed to a merciful plea from demons not to cast them out of a region and instead into the herd of swine, God can grant you mercy. You are of more value to God than demons.

> *Also, he begged Him earnestly that He would not send them out of the country. Now a large herd of swine was feeding there near the mountains. So all the demons begged Him, saying, "Send us to the swine, that we may enter them." And at once Jesus gave them permission. Then the unclean spirits went out and entered the swine (there were about two thousand), and the herd ran violently down the steep place into the sea and drowned in the sea.* (Mark 5:10-13).

Fear, intimidation, and threats

The enemy is a fake lion, and he goes around roaring like a lion to intimidate you (1 Peter 5:8). He knows that if he can make you believe he is big and scary, he can defeat you. Until you are afraid, you cannot be defeated. Ah! I tell you, the day you catch the true revelation of fear and its powerlessness over you, you will operate at a level of confidence that will shock you! Don't be deceived into thinking that just because someone threatens you,

INTERCONNECTED SYSTEMS

they have the authority and power to destroy you. A threat can be empty or, in some cases, valid and should warrant a potent response from you. The moment a person begins to threaten you, know that the battle has already started.

Do not take it lightly if the enemy dares to open his mouth to speak against you. Boldly stand up and act. The threats may come in a dream, vision or even face-to-face. Do not be afraid. The Lord reveals to redeem! Respond with words of defence and life! Elijah cowered in fear when his enemy spoke threats against his life, even though he had the power to call down fire from heaven to burn down Jezebel and all her demonic messengers.

> *And Ahab told Jezebel all that Elijah had done, also how he had executed all the prophets with the sword. Then Jezebel sent a messenger to Elijah, saying, "So let the gods do to me, and more also if I do not make your life as the life of one of them by tomorrow about this time." And when he saw that, he arose and ran for his life, and went to Beersheba, which belongs to Judah, and left his servant there.* (1 Kings 19:1-3)

I declare that any threat raised against you or those you are connected, related, or associated with in spirit and truth be cancelled now in the Name of Jesus! I speak boldness and the life of the Spirit of Christ over you now!

Goliath made the mistake of a lifetime that cost him his life! Although Goliath was trained in battle from a young age, he was no match for David. Goliath overestimated his strength and power in his fight with David (1 Samuel 17:8). He strategically issued threats as an instrument to instill fear and control. The goal was so that the people could begin to feel defeated and eventually see their defeat. If you look closely, you will see that Goliath only issued one threat multiple times, yet the people were paralyzed with fear. When the enemy issues one threat, be sure to open your mouth to issue many more to counter what he says. David opened his mouth and spoke out more than what Goliath said.

However, this cannot be done when one is empty of spiritual virtue. You cannot fight spiritual battles without spiritual power. Genuine spiritual power comes from the word of God. Therefore you must spend enough time with God, feeding your spirit regularly. For more details on how to spend time with God, please read my book, "Now That You're Born Again, What Next?" and "The Enlightened Believer." Building strength from the word is the only way the Spirit of God within you will be able to raise a standard against the enemy. It is easy to speak when you are filled. If the enemy could kill a person, he would not issue threats first. What is the devil whispering to you? So long as you apply the principles of God, nothing will have the power to touch your life.

SUCCESS SYSTEMS

God told Moses to build the tabernacle in the wilderness according to the pattern shown to him on the mountain (Exodus 25:40). There is a pattern for every desired success. Systems help with the replication of success. Some people go up and down because they have not discovered and put in an intentional system to maintain their success. There are critical aspects of life that one cannot dominate without an effective and successful system rooted in scripture. Applying these success systems will help you achieve continuous and consistent success.

Marriage Systems

A successful marriage system comprises three essential roles: the husband, wife, and spiritual authority. Spiritual authority comprises the Word of God, the person of the Holy Spirit and human authority that both the man and woman submit to. The human spiritual authority should not be the wife or husband's biological parents. These are the only roles that must be established in a successful marriage relationship and can be likened to the senior leadership team (c-suite) in an organization. Having friends or family involved in the nerve center of your relationship can cause serious issues; remove them immediately!

The process aspect of a successful marriage system addresses the day-to-day nature of marriage and the things that must be regularly fine-tuned for the marriage to work. Conflict resolution and contact (intimacy) are areas that must be visited periodically to ensure consistent success.

Communication

Many people struggle to communicate in marriage because their focus is to be heard, not to hear. You are not communicating if you are always the one talking. Communication is the ability to listen to and be heard. It is a two-way street. You must hear others out to be heard when you speak. Try this out! The next time you are conversing with your partner, reiterate what you heard them say and get their confirmation that it is accurate before you add to the conversation. Take your time to understand your partner, and watch how in due time, they take their time to understand you. But, set the right expectation so that you are not disappointed when faced with someone who doesn't care to understand and only wants to be understood. Matthew 7:12 helps us understand that we ought to do unto others what we want them to do unto us.

Keep taking the high road in communication; eventually, you will reap the reward. Another aspect to consider in the process of communication is safe communication. Avoid inflammatory communication that can demean, devalue, or derail a person emotionally. Safe communication means that you pass your point across without using words like stupid, mad, crazy, idiot, rascal, goat, snake (or other animals, other than a lion), Jezebel, Nabal, etc. Safe communication involves avoiding these inflammatory words even in a question format, like, "are you crazy?", "Are you stupid?", "Are you a goat?" etc. Asking it in a question does not excuse it. The goal of safe communication is edification, exhortation, and education. Communication should also be based on truth. Philippians 4:8 offers a list of characteristics of things to meditate on. Since out of the abundance of the heart, the mouth speaks. I encourage you to use this scripture as the basis for engaging in safe communication with your spouse. In essence, your communication should be true, noble, just, pure, lovely, have a good report, and be praiseworthy.

Conflict Resolution

Conflict resolution is about making peace, not keeping the peace. A peacekeeper avoids bringing up situations to be resolved out of fear, while a peacemaker is bold enough to bring up issues even though it might be hard sometimes. You cannot avoid conflict resolution in a marriage because there will be a need to clarify or correct words, action, or inaction. Effective conflict resolution is built on the foundational idea that the other party is a reasonable person. Your faith in your partner's ability to reason will determine the usefulness and benefit of any conflict resolution effort. There are times when a third party, like a spiritual authority, must be brought in to help with conflict resolution. While we are told not to let the sunset on our anger (Ephesians 4:26), it does not mean that every conflict needs to be resolved before the sun goes down. There is time for everything under the sun (Ecclesiastes 3), including a time for addressing conflict. The reality is that conflict is better resolved when both parties are in the right state of mind rather than when they are emotionally stirred up. Make up your mind today that you will address conflicts promptly and never keep serious issues unresolved anymore in Jesus' name. Let me also say that having conflict about big or small things in your relationship is not a sign that your relationship is heading for the rocks. Losing the desire to address issues in a marriage is a sign that the relationship is heading for the rocks.

Contact (Intimacy)

The third process in a marriage success system is contact (intimacy). Contact has to do with managing emotional, mental, physical, and spiritual intimacy. What oil is to a car is what intimacy is in a marriage relationship. The essence of intimacy is to foster and deepen a connection. 1 Corinthians 6:16 speaks to just how close in intimacy a husband and wife should be. The more genuine the contact, the deeper the intimacy and bond of love. The intimacy referred to here is physical, mental, emotional, and spiritual.

Two tools can enhance the effectiveness and efficiency of communication, conflict resolution and contact in marriage. I will address those tools here.

Joint Spiritual Engagement

Joint spiritual engagement is one of the most potent tools to be wielded for a marriage to work the way our Heavenly Father intended it to. The beauty of these spiritual tools is that it is needed in resisting demonic attempts to destroy a marriage. A marriage where the man and woman do not pray, fast, worship, attend church services and study scripture together will head for the rocks in due time.

Money

Money is a tool that must be effectively used in a marriage system. Ecclesiastes 10:19 states that money answers all things. There are many things related to living happily ever after that require money to buy. The absence of money can lead to untold suffering. And since most people do not want to suffer, a lack of money can negatively impact the ability of a couple to connect deeply. While children of God should despise the love of money, God does want us to enjoy financial prosperity. It is ok to start the marital journey without adequate financial provision but determine not to continue or end your journey without financial prosperity.

Governance

The word of God, the Holy Spirit and human spiritual authority make up the governance system that is to be over a marriage between a man and a woman. The man, however, is still the head over his home. The man being the head over the house is not a result of merit. God determined that he would empower the man in a marriage with authority to govern his home.

> *Wives, submit to your own husbands, as to the Lord. For the husband is head of the wife, as also Christ is head of the church; and He is the Savior of the body. Therefore, just as the church is subject to Christ, so let the wives be to their own husbands in everything. Husbands, love your wives, just as Christ also loved the church and gave Himself for her, that He might sanctify and cleanse her with the washing of water by the word, that He might present her to Himself a glorious church, not having spot or wrinkle or any such thing, but that she should be holy and without blemish. So, husbands ought to love their own wives as their own bodies; he who loves his wife loves himself. For no one ever hated his own flesh, but nourishes and cherishes it, just as the Lord does the church. For we are members of His body, of His flesh and of His bones. "For this reason, a man shall leave his father and mother and be joined to his wife, and the two shall become one flesh." This is a great mystery, but I speak concerning Christ and the*

church. Nevertheless, let each one of you in particular so love his own wife as himself, and let the wife see that she respects her husband. (Ephesians 5:22-33).

If your wife is taking the lead in your home, there is an imbalance and reason for concern because God has not ordained it that way. Husband, if you have differed the leadership of your home to your wife, please correct that error immediately. As a husband, you can delegate things to your wife but the overall accountability for the home rests with you. The governance system in marriage also entails the assignment of roles and responsibilities. Do your best to shun stereotypes of what tasks women traditionally do versus tasks that men traditionally do within a marriage. While assigning roles and responsibilities in a marriage, consider each party's innate gift, talents, and abilities in the home. Assigning roles within a marriage relationship encourage shared responsibility.

Financial Systems

Every successful financial system must have three critical components: consumer spending, investing, and savings. The most effective tool to use in developing and managing these three components is a budget. Budgets help to track, allocate, manage, and multiply resources.

Consumer Spending

Consumer spending has to do with exchanging money for consumption purposes like food, clothing, cars. You should not spend more on things you consume than on what you invest or save. It doesn't matter where you start, but you should focus on where you want to end. In the passage, "God gives bread to the eater and food to the sower (2 Corinthians 9:10)", we see that within every harvest that God gives us is seed for investing and sowing and bread for consumption. We have food because the farmers did not eat everything they made. No one can become financially wealthy if all their income is spent on items for consumption. Individuals classified in the low-income bracket spend more on consumption than investments or savings. In managing one's consumption, expenses must be made according to current resources, not based on others' wants or opinions. As the old saying goes, "cut your cloth according to your size, not your taste (personal emphasis added). I heard of a woman who arranged a garage sale to sell many items that she purchased but never used. The day I heard this story, I decided to consider any costly purchase for at least one day before making it.

Investments

The purpose of investing is to ensure that the future is secure. You can think of it as spending for the future. It is a mistake to say that God creates something out of nothing. An investment is a seed that God blesses for years to come. God creates something out of something. The seed you are sowing today is your opportunity for a harvest tomorrow. The little boy in John 6:12-13 who gave Jesus his lunch made an investment, which yielded enough food to feed thousands. It doesn't matter how small, set aside money for the future, invest it to generate a return of twelve baskets full of bread (John 6:12-13).

You don't have to make "enough" to put money away for investment. Your investment is not the same as savings. While savings is putting money away to be readily available for your future consumption, investment is putting money away so it can grow by working for you. Paying tithes, giving offerings, and sowing seeds to spiritual authorities are all forms of investments (Psalm 20:1-3). There was a man who Jesus granted audience because of the investments he made to the welfare of the church of God (Luke 7:5). Lydia's story is an example of a wise woman who invested so much in caring for the poor women around her (Acts 16:11;15), that it became a memorial for her when Apostle Peter was summoned to raise her back to life.

Another example was the Shunammite woman and her financial investment into Elisha, the prophet. Giving to God or God's servant must be done out of honour and respect for God, not to procure favour. Sowing into the life of the servant of God sent to you must not be done from a perspective of buying the anointing as it can backfire. Here are a few things to note about investments.

If you spend everything you are making, what will answer you on the day of trouble. Start from where you are by inputting resources aside for investments but keep desiring to do more as God blesses and uplifts you. Investments should typically start from tangible things first before intangible things. You want to start with real estate, precious metals, commodities, etc. before you should now move to intangible investments like cryptocurrency, currency or commodity trading, and the stock market. Ordinarily, the more tangible an investment, the riskier it will be. Of course, these are just principles but be open to allowing the Holy Spirit to lead you on the specifics. In the absence of specific leadings, I recommend that new investors avoid intangible assets or investments (stocks, cryptocurrency, etc.) favouring more tangible investments. The sign that you are wealthy is that the worth of your investments is more than what you earn, spend, or save.

Savings

The third aspect of a successful financial system is savings. The personal finance guru, Dave Ramsey, encourages individuals and families to have what he calls an emergency fund to use in times of emergencies instead of a credit card. We see in Proverbs 21:20 that "there is oil in the dwelling of the wise, but a foolish person squanders it." There is always an opportunity to save from whatever you are earning, like investments. Remember, Joseph's savings helped Egypt and other nations survive the seven years of famine. No matter what you are earning, there must be a plan to save, regardless of how little remains. It is not the amount that matters but that the principle is followed. Someone once said that "what you do with $100 is what you will do with $1000". It's the principle that matters. You must be diligent in little for you to be entrusted with more.

Continuous Promotion

Continuous promotion can be a reality for anyone who desires it. Proper systems, however, must be put in place to avoid stagnation. Some principles must influence the way you operate daily. Just like a human being is expected to grow so long as they eat, you are to grow and enjoy advancement as you go through life. If you are stagnant, either you are not doing what should lead to progress, the devil is resisting you, or a mixture of both. Stagnation may have been your reality but watch for there will be a shift into the realm of advancement once you begin to take the right steps. Here are some virtues to imbibe if you want to enjoy the consistent promotion.

Faithfulness

Faithfulness is the virtue that crowns a person as being worthy of trust. When a person is known and proven faithful, even God will entrust them with valuable things. When you read the parable of the talents, you see an example of faithfulness that leads to promotion.

> "So he who had received five talents came and brought five other talents, saying, 'Lord, you delivered to me five talents; look, I have gained five more talents besides them.' His lord said to him, 'Well done, good and faithful servant; you

were faithful over a few things, I will make you ruler over many things. Enter into the joy of your lord.' He also who had received two talents came and said, 'Lord, you delivered to me two talents; look, I have gained two more talents besides them.' His lord said to him, 'Well done, good and faithful servant; you have been faithful over a few things, I will make you ruler over many things. Enter into the joy of your lord.' (Matthew 25:20-23).

Symbols of promotion, such as money, power, authority, people, and resources, can only be entrusted to someone who has consistently managed such valuables that belong to others. Three servants were given five, two, and one talent, respectively; what each servant did with what was assigned to them determined their promotion or if they were demoted altogether. Whoever is faithful in little will be given much (Luke 16:10). If you want to move higher regularly, make up your mind to be consistently faithful in whatever you have been given to do.

You can show faithfulness in caring for something that does not belong to you. Scripture affirms that if you cannot be trusted with what is another man's, who will give you yours (Luke 16:12).

Goodness

A good servant is concerned about their master being blessed. A reasonable person does the right things for the right reasons. The master in the parable of talents acknowledged the first two servants as good people. You have to be a good person to want your supervisor, manager, or boss to profit regardless of how much you are paid. A good person does not wish others evil. You can never be passively good. Goodness will lead you to do good things. Goodness will lead you to desire the advancement of another, which will eventually push you to go above and beyond to ensure your responsibilities are met. Goodness will convict you when you operate under par in the actualization of your assignment. In Psalms 24:3-4, the Bible shows us that ascension is possible when we have clean hands and a pure heart and have not sworn deceitfully.

Diligence

Diligence is the grace to keep doing what you have been asked to do in and out of season. Diligence is the result of consistent discipline. Most people can temporarily discipline themselves only when something is at stake. Most students only discipline themselves to study when exams are around the corner. Diligence, however, is the consistent application of pressure towards your assignment, in season or out of season. A diligent person shows up to their assignment whether they feel like it or not. The world that God created eventually rewards diligence with promotion, whereas laziness is rewarded with involuntary labour (Proverbs 12:24).

Humility

The most critical principle in a system for continuous advancement is humility. Humility is also known as meekness. Humility is a master key that unlocks greatness in the Kingdom of God. God honours and rewards humility. However, there are different levels of humility. Jesus clarifies this in Matthew 18:4. The essence of this scripture is that humility is not a destination; instead, it is a journey. Jesus said that "whoever humbles himself as this little child is the greatest in the kingdom of heaven." (Matthew 18:4). You might already be called humble, but the real question is, "are you as humble as a little child?".

Humility requires a mindset that acknowledges someone better than you in some areas. You are not the all in all. Honouring and loving everyone you have the privilege to encounter becomes easy when you have a humbled mindset.

There is a secret to humility that many have not yet caught revelation for. The true blessing from humility does not come from being humbled, but it comes from humbling yourself in the sight of God (James 4:10). Being humbled is a form of punishment for pride and it will bring about shame. In comparison, humbling yourself is a price you willingly pay for future greatness. Do you realize here that James 4:10 did not say to only humble yourself towards God, but it says to humble yourself before God or in the presence of God? Since God is everywhere, we are to walk in humility towards everyone and everywhere. Matthew 5:5 alludes that only the meek will inherit the earth. All the great giants of faith in scripture walked in some level of humility or the other. The greatest of them all had the most humility. Jesus Christ demonstrated deep humility by taking on a service mindset and not seeing any service to God and humanity as beneath him (John 13:1-17).

The five cardinal components of humility are teachability, dependability, accountability, correctability, and identification. Teachability has to do with how open you are to learning. A humble person strives to learn from others and is not afraid to ask questions or ask for help when needed. The defendability component measures whether the individual takes it upon themselves to defend their reputation. A humble person is not preoccupied with their image. Just like when Aaron and Mariam attacked Moses' reputation, a humble person cares less about what others think about them and would not pursue the frivolity of defending their reputation. Humility also requires that a person makes themselves accountable to others.

Genuinely making yourself accountable means that you are aware of your limitations and benefit from other people's strengths. There can never be humility unless a person has genuinely submitted their outcomes to at least one authority figure in certain areas. A humble person is also correctable. The anger you feel when you are corrected is the pain from pride and signals the existence of pride. No matter how gently or lovingly you are corrected, if you feel pain or anger, it is clear that pride still exists, and it needs to be crucified. The more you subject yourself to correction, and joyfully so, the more the pride in you will die. Finally, humility involves identification. While pride seeks to stand out at all costs, humility seeks cohesion and identity. Pride likes to be separated from others, while humility makes a person want to identify with others. Moses identified with the Israelites before Pharaoh and God by calling the Israelites his people. Jesus identified with humankind by allowing Himself to be called the son of man. May the Holy Spirit help and empower you as you go deeper humility in Jesus' name.

Increase before Increase

The final component in the continuous promotion system is "increases before the increase." You cannot travel to a place in the flesh that you have not been to in the spirit or your mind. As a man thinks, so is he (Proverbs 23:7). You can tell that Joseph was already mentally out of prison and ready to rule by the speed and steps he took after being summoned by Pharaoh. The same can be said of Solomon when he requested wisdom from God. The words you confess and the actions you take are the road map to where your heart can be found. What you give your mind to meditate on will eventually produce fruits in your life. If your mind meditates on the past, then the fruit of your life will resemble the past. The same goes for meditating on the future or value-adding things like testimonies. If you trained your mind to focus on the increase you expect from God, you will find yourself beginning to take steps to prepare for the increase to come.

God shocked the Israelites with unexpected information when they were preparing to engage with the Hivites, Canaanites, and the Hittites. God told the Israelites that He would not drive their enemies out of the land they were to inhabit until they had increased enough to dominate the new territory (Exodus 23:27-30). Ask yourself this question, "If God gives you the promotion you are desiring, will you be able to manage it?" The increase God was referring to was not just in number. You must begin to increase in character, faith, spiritual capacity, mental capacity, emotional capacity, etc. In essence, begin to proactively prepare for the promotion you expect as proof that you believe God will give it to you. Complaining, stress, etc., proves that you are not ready for what you are asking for.

EPILOGUE

Children of God are expected by God to be well-grounded and well-rounded in every aspect of their lives to become all God has created for them to become. What kinds of systems have you put in place in your life? Want to implement and sustain a good new habit? Intentionally put a system in place. If you are struggling to be disciplined even after putting the system in place, I recommend that you read my book, "A Disciplined Life."

A solid system sustains everything you see around you that stands the test of time. In many cases, you will have to look very closely to see the system, while the system will be evident for you to see in other cases. Culture and tradition are systems put in place to ensure the sustenance of a group of people. What distinguishes Western Nations from other nations is mainly the systems like the rule of law, in place. Systems that determine how the citizenry will be treated, like the legal system, educational system, immigration system, etc. You cannot escape the need for a system.

I know without a doubt that you are alive at this moment because you are following a system that has kept you alive. You are at the level of success you are right now because of the systems you have adopted. Those succeeding are most likely following a different system you and I need to pay attention to. As the famous saying goes, if you fail to plan, you are planning to fail. I am telling you, however, that if you fail to put the right system in place, you are planning not to have a glorious place in the future. Your system is proof of where you see yourself in the future. Jesus said

EPILOGUE

in Luke 12:50, "but I have a baptism to be baptized with, and how distressed I am till it is accomplished!". Jesus was, in essence, saying that because of His future goals, He had to put a system in place to ensure He achieved His goals of saving humankind.

I have obeyed the guidance of the Holy Spirit to write this book because I want you to pay attention to the systems you are adopting, consciously or unconsciously. I have attempted to expose you to the importance of having suitable systems in every area of your life where you want to succeed continually. Go and succeed and may the wisdom and strength of the Father and our Lord Jesus Christ guide your steps. You have the mind of Jesus Christ! Go and continually succeed in Jesus' name.

CONTACT THE AUTHOR

I know without a doubt that this book has been a blessing to you. I am looking forward to hearing your testimony.

You can contact me through email at emmanuel.adewusi@cccghq.org or visit www.emmanueladewusi.org for more information.

A SINNER'S PRAYER

Dear Heavenly Father,

I come to You in the Name of Jesus Christ.

You said in Your Word, "Whosoever shall call upon the name of the Lord shall be saved" (Romans 10:13). I am calling on Your Name, so I know you have saved me now.

You also said that "if you confess with your mouth the Lord Jesus and believe in your heart that God has raised Him from the dead, you will be saved. For with the heart one believes unto righteousness, and with the mouth, confession is made unto salvation" (Romans 10:9-10). I believe in my heart Jesus Christ is the Son of God. I believe that He was raised from the dead for my justification, and I confess Him now as my Lord and Savior.

Thank you, Lord, because now, I am saved!

Thank You, Lord, because I know you have heard my prayer. Thank You, Lord, because I am now born again.

Signed _____

Date _____

ABOUT THE AUTHOR

Emmanuel Adewusi is the Founding and Lead Pastor of Cornerstone Christian Church of God.

Called into ministry with the mandate to "bring restoration and transformation to all by teaching, preaching and demonstrating the gospel of Jesus Christ," he is passionate to see lives restored and transformed the way God intended from the beginning of creation. He has a passion for the full counsel of the word of God, fellowship with the Holy Spirit and being under spiritual authority.

He hosts several *"Come and See"* Conferences, with the goal to reach lost souls for Jesus Christ.

He authored the books *"Now That You Are Born Again, What Next?"*, *"The Blessings of Being Under Spiritual Authority,"* "A Disciplined Life," *"Channels of Grace: How to Seamlessly Connect & Stay Connected with God"* and other impactful titles. He has also released an album titled *"Divine Encounter"* and many more on the way.

Emmanuel Adewusi is joyfully married to his wife, Ibukun Adewusi, and together, they are building a thriving Christ-centered family.